NATHANAEL GREENE *in* SOUTH CAROLINA

Hero of the AMERICAN REVOLUTION

LEIGH M. MORING

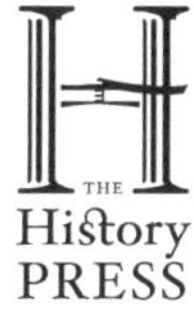

Published by The History Press
Charleston, SC
www.historypress.net

Cover images: *The Battle of Eutaw Springs*, steel engraving depicting General Greene pointing his army onward on the morning of September 8, 1781. Original painting by Chappel, published by Johnson, Fry and Company in New York, 1859. *Courtesy of the Library of Congress*; painting of Nathanael Greene by Robert Wilson. *Courtesy of Robert Wilson Fine Art.*

First published 2016

Manufactured in the United States

ISBN 978.1.46713.686.0

Library of Congress Control Number: 2016948311

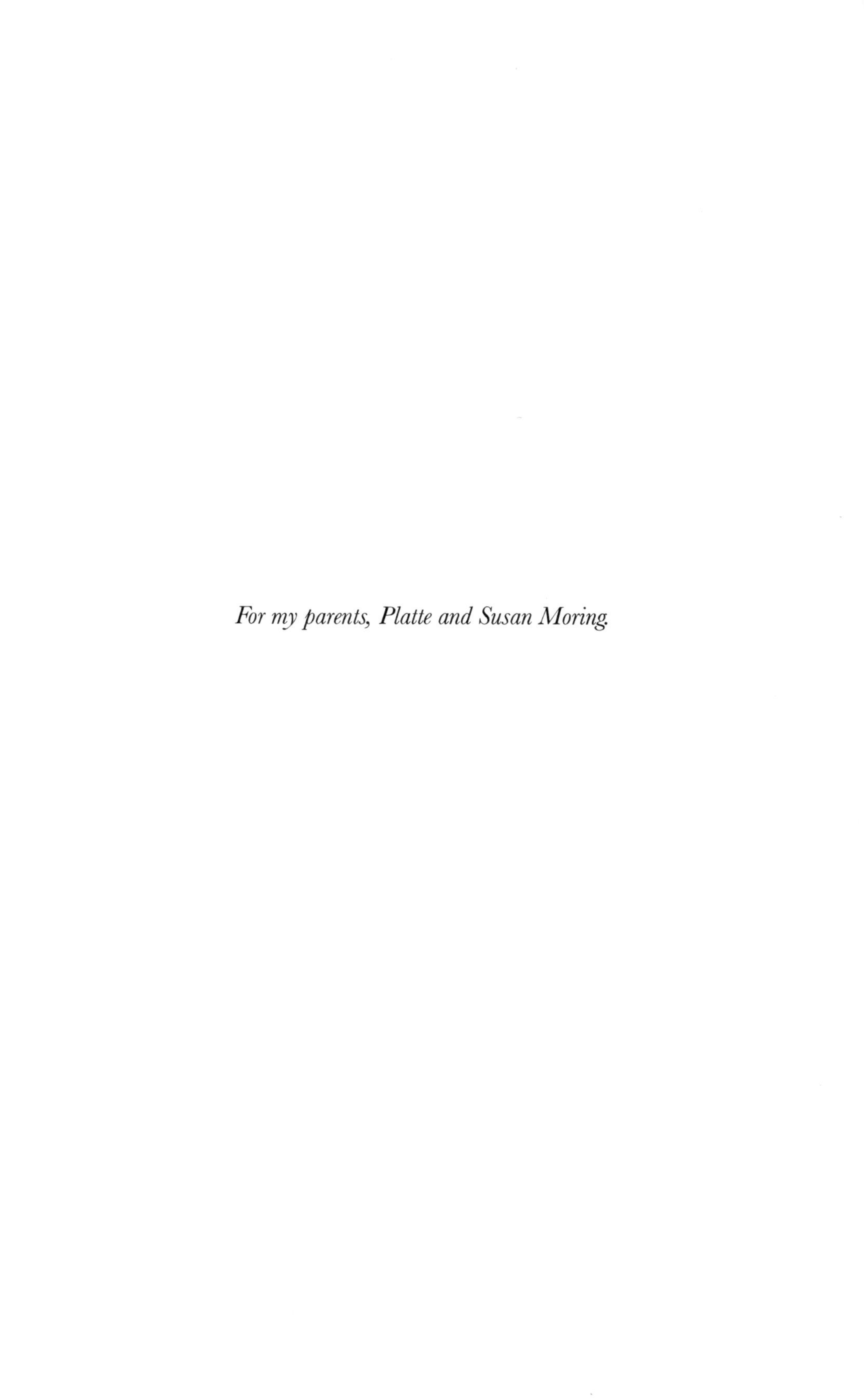

For my parents, Platte and Susan Moring.

CONTENTS

PREFACE

Nathanael Greene assumed command of the southern campaigns during the American Revolution following previous failed leadership in December 1780. George Washington charged Greene with removing the British from the South, which he was ultimately able to do, but not until 1783. In this book, discover Greene's operations in South Carolina with a focus on the events that directly led to his liberation of Charleston in 1782 and the struggles he faced in achieving this feat—a final victory that involved much toil, tears and sweat, but one that he achieved with little bloodshed. Historians and educators tend to overlook the period from the British Surrender at the Battle of Yorktown on October 19, 1781, to the evacuation of Charleston in December 1782, so this book fills a gap in the existing chronicles of the period and presents new findings. Greene dealt with supply and manpower shortages, faced Loyalists and liberated slave units fighting for the British and met opposition from his peers in the political dealings of South Carolina. This book introduces a new perspective on an important period in Greene's command by explaining how the Revolutionary War really ended. Readers should note that until Charleston was incorporated as an American city on August 13, 1783, the city was called Charles Town. The name was changed to remove traces of its ties to Britain. For the purpose of clarity, the city will be referred to by its modern name of Charleston in this book, but Greene and his contemporaries would have written and called it Charles Town before that date in 1783.

ACKNOWLEDGEMENTS

There are many people I would like to thank for helping me with the publication of my first book. First, I want to thank Dr. David Preston. Dr. Preston was my graduate thesis advisor at The Citadel. I came to Dr. Preston wanting to write about one of my personal heroes, Francis Marion, but he suggested I take a look at Nathanael Greene. He recommended books to use for research and was always happy to listen to any theories and new information I had found in Greene's papers. Dr. Preston was a wonderful thesis advisor and encouraged me to lengthen and publish my thesis into a book.

The staff at my place of business, Historic Charleston Foundation, has been great throughout this whole process. Their support during this journey is much appreciated.

As the Education Coordinator for Historic Charleston Foundation, I have the privilege of working with many historic sites and museums in the Charleston area. I am grateful for the interest and excitement that many of these educational professionals have shown in this project and their willingness to assist me. In particular, Jennifer McCormick at The Charleston Museum was helpful, as she allowed me to examine actual correspondence between Greene and his contemporaries from the museum archives. Also, John Young at the Powder Magazine served as my expert on Charleston and answered many historical questions that came up in my research.

Lastly, I would like to thank my parents, Platte and Susan Moring, for encouraging me to pursue my interest in history from a young age. Family trips to historical sites fed my passion and fueled my desire to learn all I could about the past. My parents made my education possible, so I really owe this book to them. I also want to thank my friends Brittany Tolleson, Callie Neal, Manning Mullikin, Eva Cheros and Casey Anne Attaway for their support and encouragement. I am truly grateful for all of my family, friends, past teachers and colleagues, for they have all had a hand in this project.

INTRODUCTION

We have been beating the bush and the General has come to catch the bird.
–Greene on the impending surrender at Yorktown

On September 29, 1781, Major General Nathanael Greene wrote from South Carolina to his friend Henry Knox, who was in Virginia with General Washington. The French and American armies had begun to besiege Lord Charles Cornwallis's British forces at Yorktown. Greene encouraged Knox that "the prospect is so bright and the glory so great that I want you to be there to share in them."[1] Although everyone seemed transfixed on the Siege of Yorktown, Greene had already earned his own laurels in the Carolinas. Greene would not be present at Cornwallis's surrender, but he certainly deserved credit for exhausting the British army and sending it toward eventual defeat in Virginia. But before Greene could rest and enjoy the new country he was liberating, he first had to handle the still-powerful British army that remained in South Carolina. The first step in that process was the clash at Eutaw Springs in September 1781, the last major battle of the war in the state, which was pivotal in pushing the British back to Charleston.

Earlier that month, Greene had just taken his army from its encampment at Burdall's Plantation and marched toward Eutaw Springs. Before this march, Greene's mission was to end British control in the South Carolina upcountry, starting with recapturing the town of Ninety-Six. Greene felt that this might be the final offensive of the Revolutionary War in South Carolina. For the entire month of May 1781, Greene and his men laid siege to that fortified village. Only after he learned that more British reinforcements were landing in Charleston did he assault the fort and retreat to Charlotte. Lord Rawdon, the British commander, heavily pursued Greene for several days. Greene was used to evading the British, and he knew he could tire out his opponents through his usual strategy of long marches. Just as Greene expected, Rawdon and his men were exhausted by the pursuit and had to retire to Charleston, where Rawdon left command of his forces to British Colonel Alexander Stewart.

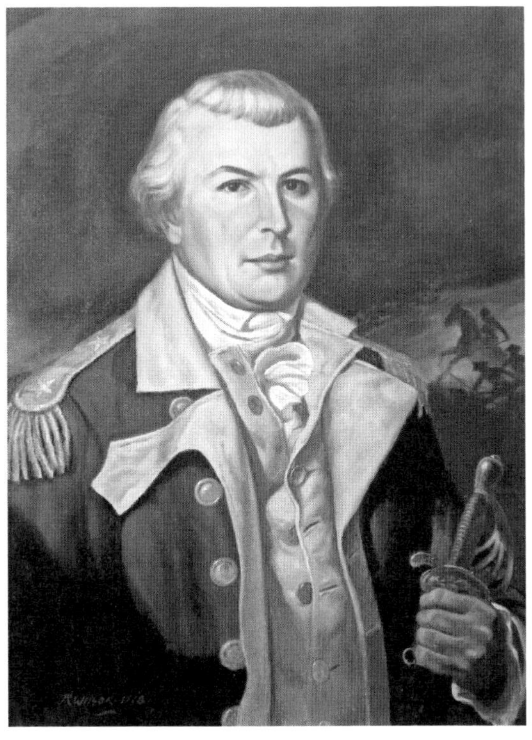

Painting of Nathanael Greene by Robert Wilson. *Courtesy of Robert Wilson Fine Art.*

Greene decided at this point to head toward Charleston as well to face the remaining British forces, all garrisoned in one of the last British-occupied southern towns. Stewart and his two thousand men were in search of Greene and left Charleston to meet them on their way. They camped at Eutaw Springs just seven miles from where Greene was marching on that fateful September day in 1781. Greene had the weight of the Revolution in the South on his shoulders, and he had grown weary of the war's destruction. He often thought of his wife at home in Rhode Island and wrote as much as he could to her. Nathanael had married Catharine "Caty" Littlefield in 1774 and had five children with her. He knew that she had her own hardships in raising the children and managing the finances on her own. But he knew it was his duty to his country to continue fighting with Washington. He wrote to Caty:

> *I suppose you are at Westerly. I wish I was there with you, free from the bustle of the World and the miseries of war. My nature recoils at the horrid scenes which this Country affords, and longs for a peaceful retirement where love and, softer pleasures are to be found. Here turn which way you will,*

> *you hear nothing but mournful widow, and plantations laid waste. Ruin is in every form and misery in every shape. The heart you sent me is in my Watch, and your picture in my bosom.*[2]

Greene tried to suppress his feelings of misery and focus on his task at hand. He woke his men up early on September 8, 1781, and started them marching from Burdall's Plantation near Eutaw. The British were also up early that morning. Stewart had sent a few hundred of his men out of Eutaw Springs to forage for food. They found a beautiful forest of cypress and oak trees with an underground river that burst into two springs. The cool springs drained into Eutaw Creek, which flowed straight into the Santee River. Stewart's men stopped to admire the beauty of South Carolina around the woods of their campsite on the property of a three-story brick mansion. Their rows of tents housing about 1,900 troops dotted the clearing behind the mansion like neatly planted crops. The British found some sweet potatoes growing in the ground.[3]

While the foraging party was digging, Nathanael Greene's army was marching slowly toward them. Covering only about three miles in three hours, they were creeping along as slowly as the Santee River's morning mist. Greene knew that they could use some encouragement, as Greene's tent mate and friend Colonel Otho Williams wrote, "We moved in order of battle about three miles, when we halted, and took a little of that Liquid which is not unnecessary to exhillarate the Chimiral Spirits upon such occasions. Again we advanced, and soon afterwards our light troops met the van of the enemy, who were marching out to meet us."[4]

After the brief stop for rum, Williams thought they had met the British forward troops—or van, as he calls it—but really it was just the unarmed sweet potato party, which they quickly captured. In the distance, booms of muskets sounded like deathly explosions in the woods of oak on a hot morning. The two advancing parties eventually met at Eutaw Springs, where Greene said "a most tremendous firing began."[5] Cannonballs blasted through the woods and shook the ground where Greene and his men were standing. This time he was ready; his militia had the experience of battle and fired off several rounds per man before being driven back into the woods by the advancing British.

The Americans returned the favor and pushed forward with their more experienced men from North Carolina, driving the Redcoats back to their camp. Greene's Continental troops continued the advance, and the British retreated through their own neat lines of tents. They dashed toward the big

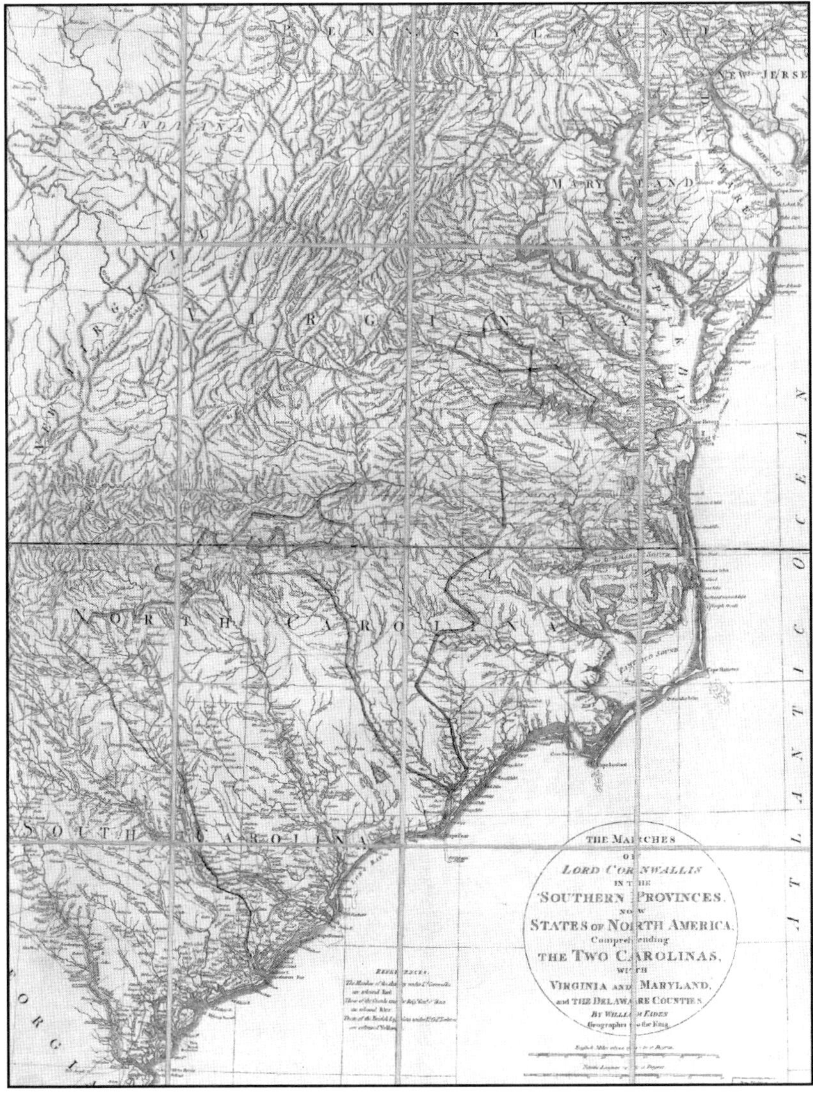

The marches of Lord Cornwallis in the southern states. By William Faden (1749–1836). Published in London 1787. *Courtesy of Library of Congress.*

mansion, thinking that the walled garden would be a good place to occupy against the enemy. Greene's men, realizing what they were doing, raced against the British, trying to get inside the mansion first. Although the British troops won, the Americans' consolation prize was plundering their enemy's tents for food and drink. Fine liquor, food and clothing, however, distracted the troops from danger looming overhead. British marksmen opened fire from the mansion's windows on the Americans below with deadly blasts. Williams commented on the scene unfolding:

> *Everything now combined to blast the prospects of the American commander. The fire from the house showered down destruction upon the American officers; and the men perhaps thinking the victory secure and bent on the immediate fruition of its advantages, dispersing among the tents, fastened upon the liquors and became completely unmanageable.*[6]

Greene's men had become entrapped in the bushes near the river by the mansion, and the British quickly overtook them. One of the American commanders, Colonel William Washington, was bayoneted and captured. Four hours of fighting later, Greene pulled back, feeling stymied but not defeated. He had his men walk the seven miles back to Burdall's Plantation, where they had camped the night before, to get some rest and food before the next day of battle. When Greene returned to the site of the battle, he found that the British had left for Charleston, not claiming the field that they had just taken. Greene penned more details about the Battle of Eutaw Springs. On September 9, 1781, Greene claimed victory in a letter to the governor of South Carolina, writing, "We have had a most obstinate and bloody action. Victory was ours."[7]

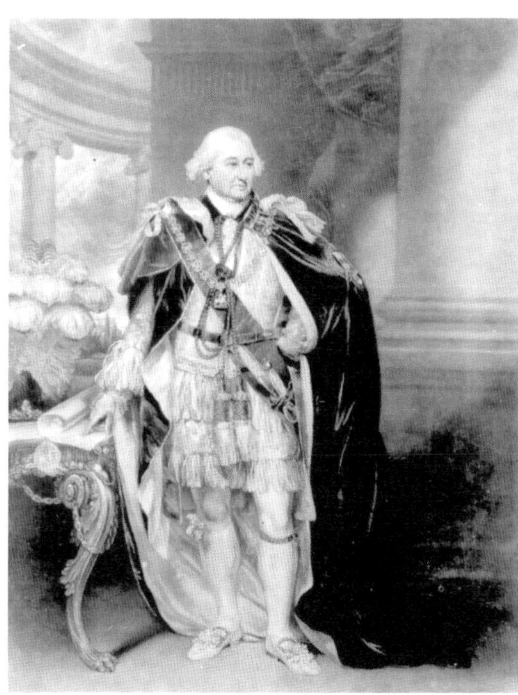

Lord Cornwallis. Engraving (full length) by J. Ward from painting by Sir W. Beechey, published in 1799. *Courtesy of the National Archives.*

British General Stewart later heard that Greene had claimed victory and became furious, writing that *he* had been victorious in the battle and wanting to be promoted to brigadier general following this victory.

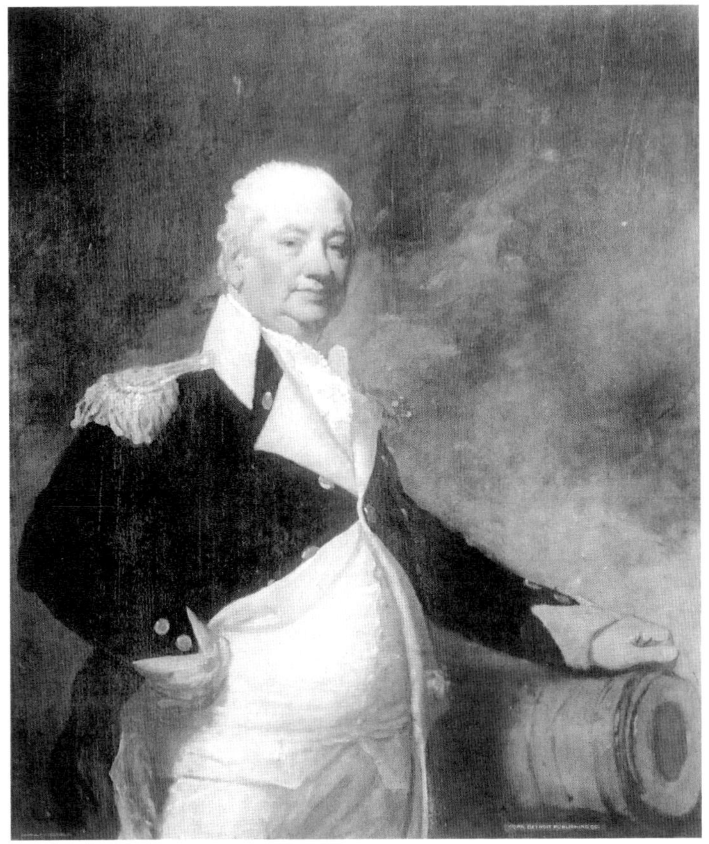

Major General Henry Knox, painted by Gilbert Stuart (1755–1828). *Courtesy of Library of Congress.*

Although the battle had ended, both commanders were still warring over who had actually won the Battle of Eutaw Springs. Even the total number of casualties on both sides was debated, as the British reported 85 dead, 351 wounded and 257 missing, but Greene reported that he had captured 500 prisoners, 70 of whom were wounded. On the American side, three separate reports came in with different numbers, but the final revision stated 139 dead, 375 wounded and 78 missing, with 70 taken prisoner.[8] A quarter of Greene's force had been lost, while 40 percent of Stewart's men were gone. "As for who won, arguably the 'honors' of that day belonged to Stewart as his troops camped on the field; but as in all of Nathanael Greene's so-called defeats, he won by losing."[9] This had become a pattern for Greene, as he often technically lost battles to the British but gained ground and pushed them ultimately toward Charleston. Stewart marched his men from Eutaw Springs to the outskirts of Charleston on September 9 and left 70 wounded men in addition to some broken supplies and rum casks. Seizing his opportunity carefully, Greene pursued the British troops all the way to Fergusons Swamp, which was just thirty miles outside Charleston.

This chase was probably one of the most significant things that happened toward the end of the war, as Greene essentially pushed all the remaining British in South Carolina into Charleston, which would eventually be the last major city they occupied before abandoning the continent and sailing back to England. Stewart's men met up with British reinforcements, causing Greene to break off and eventually return to the High Hills of the Santee, but not before stopping back at Eutaw Springs. The American army returned to River Road in the morning to observe the battlefield and reflect before its march into the High Hills. Greene contemplated the battle that had just taken place and thought of his family, his Rhode Island home, the loss of life and the impending end of the war, which he felt was near. Greene was correct: the British would surrender at Yorktown in October, but Greene's work would not be done for another year.

Greene's task of fully liberating South Carolina and pushing the British out of Charleston was a campaign that lasted until December 1782. While most history books portray Cornwallis's surrender at Yorktown as the end of hostilities in the Revolutionary War, Greene's war in South Carolina continued for another fifteen months. It was not until December 1782 that Greene and the Continental army finally marched down the streets of Charleston in triumph as the British evacuated South Carolina forever. How Greene achieved this final victory over the British after the Battle of Eutaw Springs remains an untold story. The issue that defined Greene's command of the South since the time he arrived in December 1780 was the state of his troops.

The men were poorly clothed, fed, equipped and behaved. They did not take orders well, some were not well trained and their spirits and morale were always low due to the poor conditions under which they were living. After taking command, Greene quickly fixed the discipline problem, but his troops would be badly equipped for the remainder of the war. Additionally, his hospital supplies were never what they should have been. Sometimes his men who fought valiantly in battles would survive only to die from infected and untreated wounds. This fact outraged Greene, who wrote constantly to George Washington and Congress asking for provisions to be sent. He often visited Patriot hospitals and remarked on the saddening conditions the soldiers dealt with while in care.

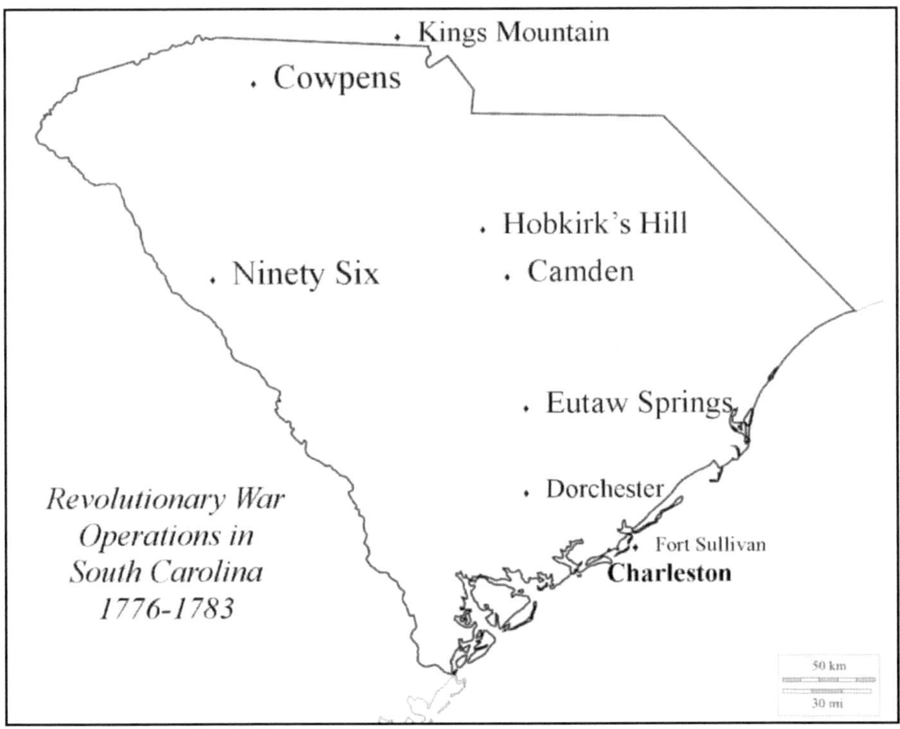

Map of South Carolina depicting some of the major military engagements in the state during the American Revolution. *Map created by author.*

Greene not only struggled with proper supplies for his men but also lacked the proper number of infantry and cavalry suitable for battle. Immediately following the Battle of Eutaw Springs, Greene was worried that Cornwallis would send reinforcements down to Stewart and that they would attempt to recapture more of South Carolina. Greene begged for reinforcements of his own but would not receive any. There was still the problem of ridding the Carolinas of remaining Loyalists. The British had a victory in North Carolina, which lifted their morale and subsequently caused a number of uprisings. Greene was able to defeat the last remaining Tory groups in the Pee Dee region, but controversy followed. Greene wished to handle the Loyalists moderately, but others did not like his merciful approach toward their actions.

After the British surrendered at Yorktown in mid-October, more problems began for Greene. His issues of dwindling soldiers, few provisions and low spirits only intensified after the surrender. The militia left the ranks shortly after Cornwallis's announcement, and some of Greene's generals were sent elsewhere. The number of Continentals Greene had in his command was reduced drastically as well. Although they had surrendered, the British were still posing a threat to Greene in the Carolinas and were stationed in Charleston with no intention of leaving just yet. Always fearful of retaliation, Greene needed to force the consolidation of the remaining Redcoats into one place and push them down into the neck of Charleston. Greene began to mobilize his remaining troops and headed toward Charleston. The mere rumor that Greene was on his way sent a panic through the British, and they all went to Fort Dorchester, one of their last remaining posts, just as Greene had hoped they would. In December 1781, the Americans engaged with the British in a few skirmishes outside the fort. Once Greene had been sighted, the British commander panicked, destroyed everything at the fort and fled rather than face Greene and his army. They moved down to the neck of Charleston and the surrounding areas, where they stayed on the defensive for most of the next year.

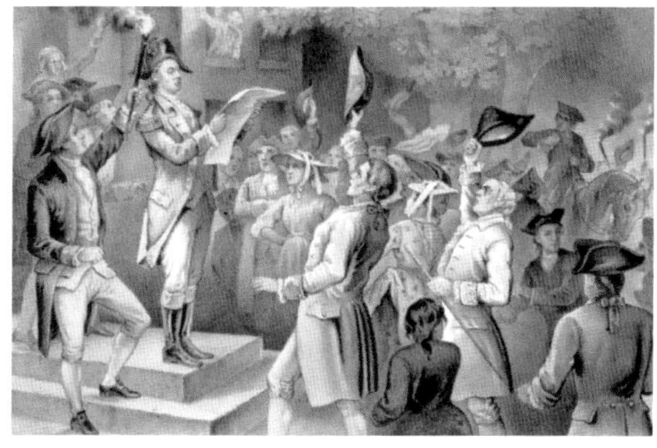

Lieutenant Colonel Tighlman of Washington's staff announces the surrender of Cornwallis from the steps of Independence Hall in Philadelphia on October 23, 1781. Published by Currier & Ives, 1876, in New York. *Courtesy of Library of Congress.*

Greene got very involved in politics in 1782 while he had the British mostly bottled up in Charleston. He constantly wrote in support of a strong national government; more provisions and care for the Patriot army, which had served many years; and more attention paid to the situation still at hand in the South. He reminded Americans that the war was still going on and that the British were still dangerous and posing a constant and dangerous threat in Charleston. Even South Carolinians became more passive about the situation despite the British seizing slaves to fight. They felt that the British were weak and not a formidable opponent any longer since the surrender. Greene was still characteristically worried and strongly encouraged a sitting legislature to meet just outside Charleston to try to scare the British into leaving. The Americans and British still skirmished from time to time, one in particular taking the life of a key Patriot, but it was mostly to prevent the British from stealing provisions from Americans.

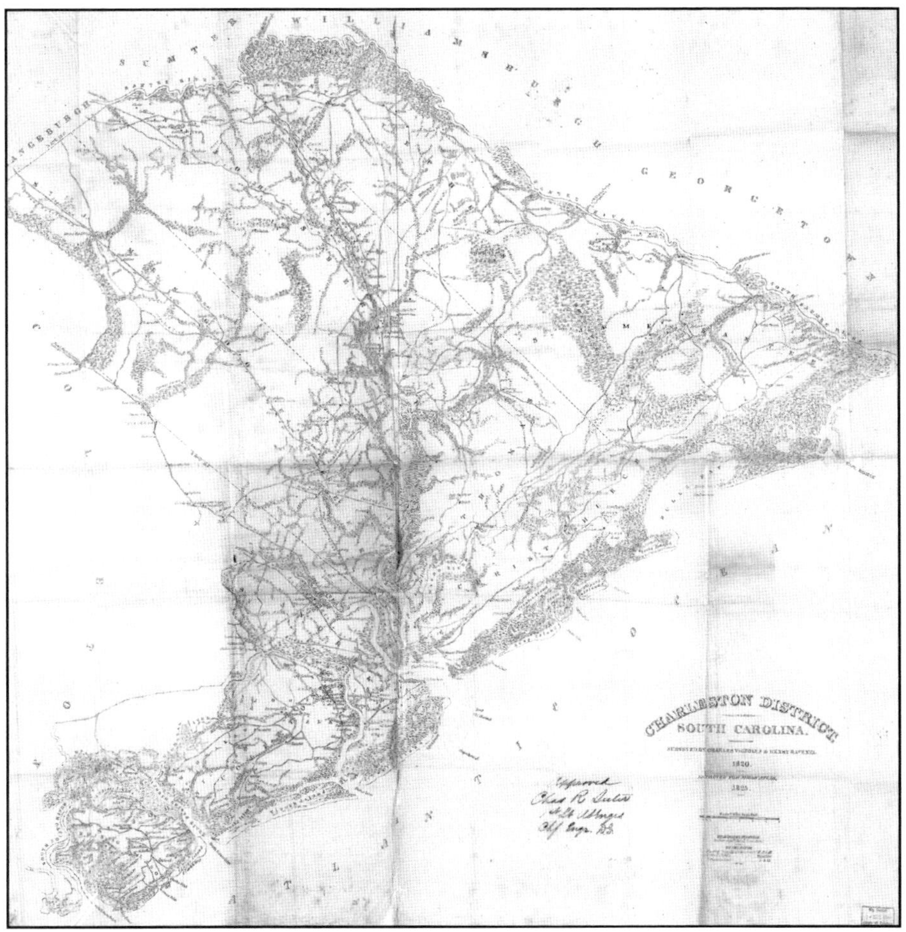

Map of Charleston District, South Carolina, by Robert Mills. *Courtesy of Library of Congress.*

Eventually, the British did leave Charleston, and Greene and his men were able to march down the streets of the newly liberated city in triumph, but not without issue. Greene's command of the southern campaigns was a success but marked with the same problems throughout, and it took him a while to accomplish his goals. None of his victories was technically a win, but they all succeeded in his moving the British down to the coast of the state. Existing literature tends to focus more on the sensational parts of his command, such as the series of battles in the upcountry that occurred in the beginning of his command. This work will detail Greene's operations in South Carolina with a focus on the events that directly led to his liberation of Charleston in 1782 and the struggles he faced in achieving this feat.

Chapter 1

"KNOWLEDGE WITHOUT INTEGRITY IS DANGEROUS AND DREADFUL"

Learning is not virtue but the means to bring us an acquaintance with it. Integrity without knowledge is weak and useless, and knowledge without integrity is dangerous and dreadful. Let these be your motives to action through life, the relief of the distressed, the detection of frauds, the defeat of oppression, and diffusion of happiness.

—Greene on education

The American Revolution is a topic that interests many historians and the general public alike because it was the war in which America won its independence. Icons like George Washington, Benedict Arnold, Benjamin Franklin and Thomas Jefferson tend to garner much of the attention. However, historians have investigated many other Patriots—ordinary people, women and blacks, as well as long-neglected military figures who had extensive contributions to American independence. Nathanael Greene is one such Patriot, who was actually known as George Washington's most gifted and dependable officer. He is the most important Revolutionary War general that you probably do not know.

Why have you not heard of Greene before? Only recently have historians reported on his major role in battles during the American Revolution. Now scholarship on Greene is increasingly accessible thanks to the hard work of Dennis Conrad, who edited the entire collection of Nathanael Greene's papers and published them in thirteen chronological volumes. His contribution is extremely significant because historians can access all of

Greene's correspondences and personal papers in one place. Now it is possible for researchers to get further into the mind of Nathanael Greene and discover the military genius and character of Washington's most trusted officer.

Some of the items in the papers are correspondence, letters, militia lists and military reports. Many biographies and battlefield histories have been published about Greene and the southern campaigns, but these volumes allow for greater depth and detail on this topic. Conrad has edited his volumes in a skilled way that allows for a clear and chronological narrative of Greene's life to be studied. He includes notes and references that clarify what Greene wrote about particular battles or situations. But who is Greene, and how did he save the South?

This book focuses on the liberation of South Carolina and Charleston, from Greene taking command of the Southern Army in 1781 until the final British evacuation on December 14, 1782. This study will fill a gap in our knowledge of exactly how Greene was able to achieve final victory, a process that previous historians have assumed and not explained in depth. That omission has obscured the importance of Greene's strategy and political moves that actually removed the British from Charleston in 1782. Nathanael Greene was one of the driving forces behind the British evacuating the Lowcountry of South Carolina, as his army posed a constant threat to the British occupation and they regarded Greene and his military capability highly. He prevailed over the British in Charleston despite the fact that, at times, they had three times the manpower that Greene had.

To fully appreciate Greene's final victory in 1782, it is necessary to understand Greene's background and character and the conditions he faced when starting as commander of the southern campaigns. Nathanael Greene was an unlikely American hero and warrior who was able to take inexperienced officers, untrained volunteer militia men and virtually no supplies and still win a war.

Greene was born into a Quaker family who hated war and did not believe in education past reading and writing. He walked with a limp and did not see war until the Siege of Boston in 1775, but he had already been made a general. How Greene was given command of Rhode Island's army is a bit of a mystery. He was a merchant, tradesman and indeed a Patriot but certainly not qualified to be a general before he had even tasted conflict and experienced the military.

Greene's lack of a formal education is one of the most important parts of his character. Born in Coventry, Rhode Island, in August 1742 to Quaker parents, Greene was keen to learn despite his father's wishes and religion, so

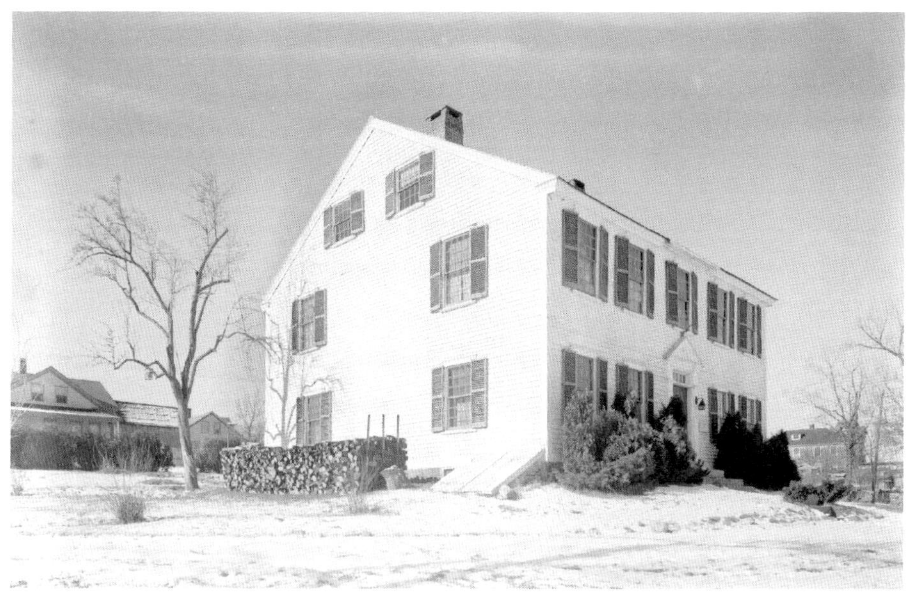

General Nathanael Greene's home in Coventry, Rhode Island. Historic American Buildings Survey. *Courtesy of Library of Congress.*

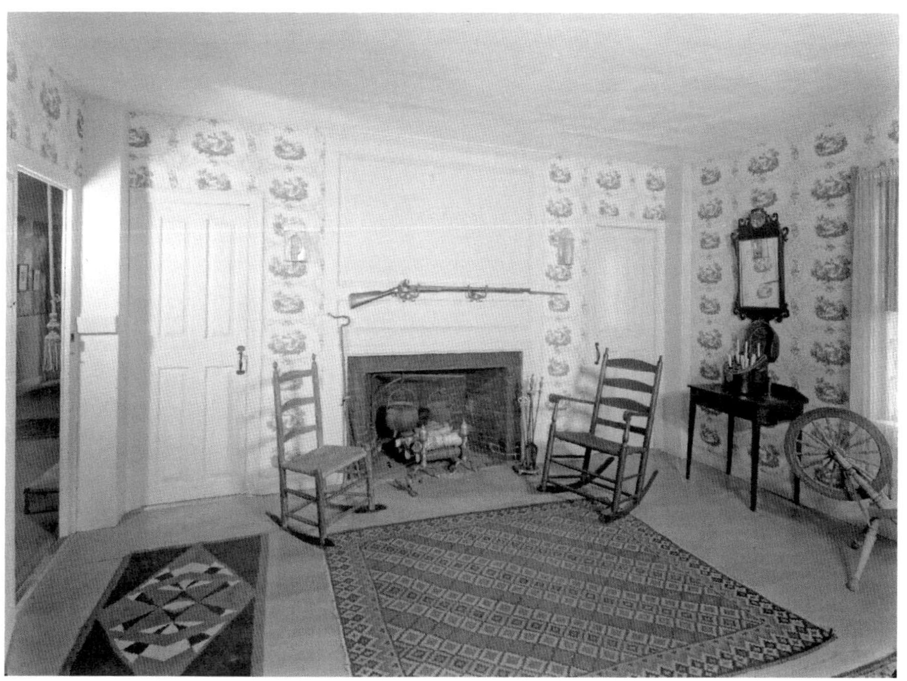

Nathanael Greene's home in Coventry. Dining room is pictured. Historic American Buildings Survey. *Courtesy of Library of Congress.*

he taught himself the fundamentals of a basic education. He also took an academic interest in the art of war. He spent time reading military classics by Julius Caesar and Frederick the Great. Greene was the first in his Rhode Island town to push for the establishment of a public school in 1770. In that same year, he was chosen to be a member of the Rhode Island General Assembly and continued to serve up until the outbreak of the Revolutionary War. His commitment and dedication to his own education and his early involvement in politics are what led him to enlist in the local militia. He was just a private in a unit called the Kentish Guards. Greene's participation in the militia was challenged, as he had a clear limp in his walk that he had had since birth. Greene stood out not because of his leadership ability but because of that limp. It was quite noticeable when the entire group was out on parade in East Greenwich.

Determined to overcome and prove himself, he continued to read extensive volumes on the art of war to learn military tactics. He rose to be one of the leaders of the group and worked with the legislative assembly to revise militia laws. Because of his passion for the militia and fighting the British, the Quakers expelled him from their Order. In 1774, Greene married Catharine "Caty" Littlefield, with whom he would have five children. Caty and Nathanael's honeymoon phase was cut short, as he was called to war less than a year after their marriage. She was fiercely loyal throughout Greene's military career, although she only wished that he could be home with her and the children. Caty often dreamed of spending winter nights together, reading by the fireplace.[10] Her letters to Nathanael are what kept him going in the tough days of the war, and her visits to him at his headquarters were always welcome.

In 1775, Greene was promoted from private to major general of the Rhode Island Army of Observation, which was formed because of the situation in Boston. This overnight promotion could have been due to his family's political connections[11] or possibly because he had a forceful personality. Either way, Greene found himself as the commanding general before he had even heard a cannon explode or experienced an enemy charging at him. "The appointment had consequences for the army and for the nation that Rhode Island's lawmakers could not have imagined. Had he not been given command of his colony's home troops, he very likely would not have become the Continental army's youngest brigadier general."[12] Later, the Continental Congress made him a brigadier of the Continental army, and Washington personally appointed him as commander of Boston once the British had evacuated in March 1776. Had Greene not become a brigadier general, he would not have come to George Washington's attention and certainly not so early in the war. Greene would become Washington's most trusted general, all thanks to some Rhode Island lawmakers who had the foresight, but not a good reason, to promote him.

While Greene's appointment from private to general in Rhode Island remains a mystery, his rise in the Continental army was certainly not. Greene shined as an expert on military strategy, a strong and capable leader and an organized and persistent fighter. Congress quickly promoted him later that year to the rank of major general, where he continued to prove himself as a capable commander to Washington in his involvement in campaigns in New York, Philadelphia and Rhode Island up until 1780. Greene had been with Washington during the liberation of Boston, retreat through New Jersey, defeats at Germantown and Brandywine, rough winter at Valley Forge, victory at Monmouth and the snow in Morristown.[13] Under Washington, Greene offered strategic advice, commanded troops and served in the thankless role of quartermaster. He hated this job of ordering and transporting supplies, but he did it. Greene had left behind a successful business and beautiful bride as a thirty-three-year-old to join this war as an ardent Patriot but also a man yearning for fame and fortune. He hoped that the war could provide both for himself and for his family. It looked like he was destined for neither at first; Greene would just be another volunteer who answered his country's call and was merely another general on Washington's staff. He even told Washington that history does not remember quartermaster generals.

All of his childhood spent reading books on war strategy had given him the desire to lead troops at war. He became even more upset after his enemy following the Battle of Saratoga, Horatio Gates, had been named commander of the Southern Department. Greene had been Washington's pick, but he was overruled in favor of Gates. However, Greene would have his chance, as the Southern Army was shattered under the command of Gates. The disastrous southern campaigns culminated in an embarrassing loss in Camden, South Carolina, in the summer of 1780 in which the Continental army lines broke and ran in wild confusion, ending the Southern Army's cohesion. Cornwallis easily gathered Loyalists, took the fighting to Virginia and used the southern ports of Savannah and Charleston to move men and supplies into the interior of the Carolinas.

The Continental army had seen many crushing defeats since 1775, and Greene had been present for them all. The worst was in 1780. A horrible winter in New Jersey, worthless currency, surrender at Charleston and annihilation at Camden made victory seem a distant wish. Greene had personal struggles

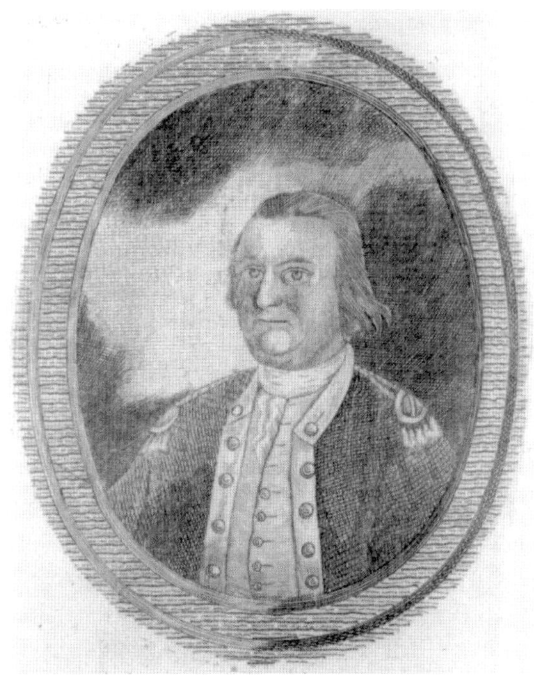

Major General Benjamin Lincoln etched by John Norman (1748–1817). *Courtesy of Library of Congress.*

with an ill wife and son in Rhode Island and his own health issues due to asthma.

In the fall, the Americans' fortunes took another downturn. Greene's friend Benedict Arnold made his infamous move and almost was able to give West Point to the British. The American cause was close to being lost, and a shift in command in the South was about to take place. Congress had made two poor decisions in Benjamin Lincoln, major general of the Continental army, and Gates. It was time to finally listen to a military mastermind.

Washington only had one man in mind when it came to choosing the new commander of the Southern Army to replace Major General Gates. He quickly sent Greene, who was at West Point, a short but profound request: "It is my wish to appoint you."[11] Greene wanted Gates's job despite the bleak situation in the South. He did not think

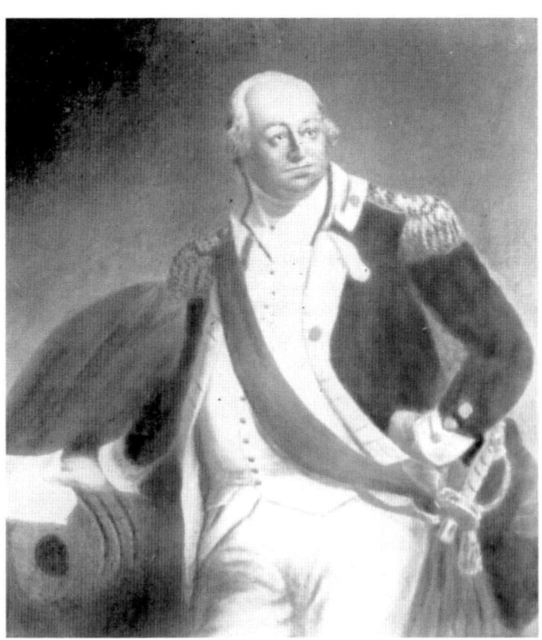

Benjamin Lincoln, painting (3/4 length) by Henry Sargent. *Courtesy of the National Archives.*

it would be him, as he had just taken over Benedict Arnold's command of West Point. When Washington wrote and requested he go south immediately, Greene realized that this was the chance for great power but at an impossible cost. Cornwallis was attempting to cut the new country in half, and it was up to him to stop the march north. But Greene always answered when duty called, so he accepted and became second in command only to Washington himself, with power over all troops from Delaware to Georgia. Greene did not get the chance to say goodbye to his wife and now four children before he made the trek South. He assumed his post on December 2, 1780, in Charlotte, North Carolina. The fate of the nation was on his shoulders, and if he failed, all would be lost.

Greene was just a simple Quaker from Rhode Island "who abandoned his religious upbringing and strived to learn more than only what he found in his own backyard."[15] Greene was alone in the struggle to rid the southern shores of the British, and for two years, he fought hard and skillfully to ultimately emerge victorious. At the end of the war, Greene exited from the public stage despite his contemporaries begging him to enter politics. He decided to live out the rest of his short life on his plantation in Georgia with his family. Perhaps if he had not died prematurely, America might better know Greene's name.

Before Greene took his role as commander of the Southern Army, much was happening in South Carolina. A little-known fact is that there were more battles of the American Revolution in South Carolina than in any other state. The very first battle came a week before the Declaration was signed in Philadelphia. On June 28, 1776, the British sailed toward the Charleston Harbor in hopes to take the city as its own. Sir Henry Clinton and Commodore Peter Parker originally intended to support the Loyalists of North Carolina but got word that Patriots had dispersed them earlier in February. Clinton shifted his focus to South Carolina, as he hoped he could establish a base there for Loyalists to seek refuge. He set his sights on Sullivan's Island. This small sea island would be the perfect spot, as it guarded the entrance to the Charleston Harbor, the wealthiest colonial port city.[16]

Under the command of Colonel William Moultrie, Fort Sullivan had been constructed out of sand and palmetto tree logs and was located on the southern tip of the island. However, the fort had not been finished by the time the British arrived in Charleston. Clinton and his men landed just north of Charleston on June 16, 1776, on Long Island, now called Isle of Palms. Their plan was twofold: Parker would hit the fort from the ocean, and troops would enter the island from the northern end by way of Breach Inlet. On

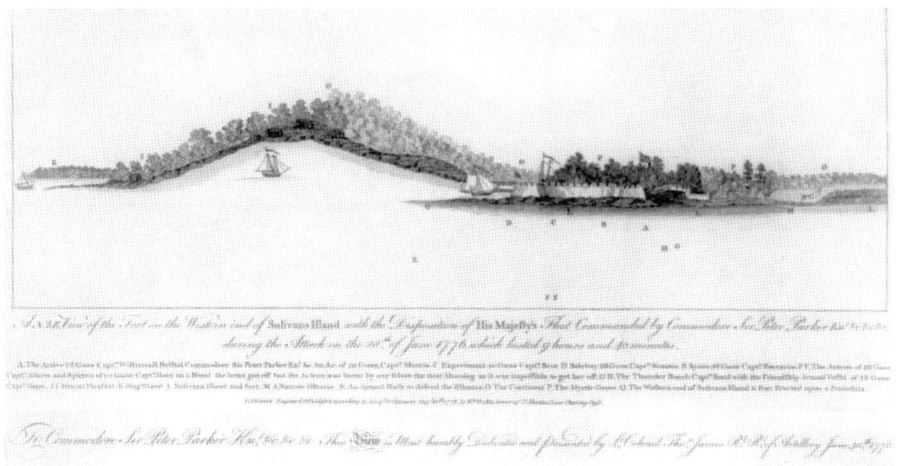

Print by William Fadden (1749–1836) showing Sullivan's Island at the entrance to Charleston Harbor. Published in London to depict the Battle of Fort Sullivan between Commodore Sir Peter Parker's fleet and the South Carolinians. *Courtesy of Library of Congress.*

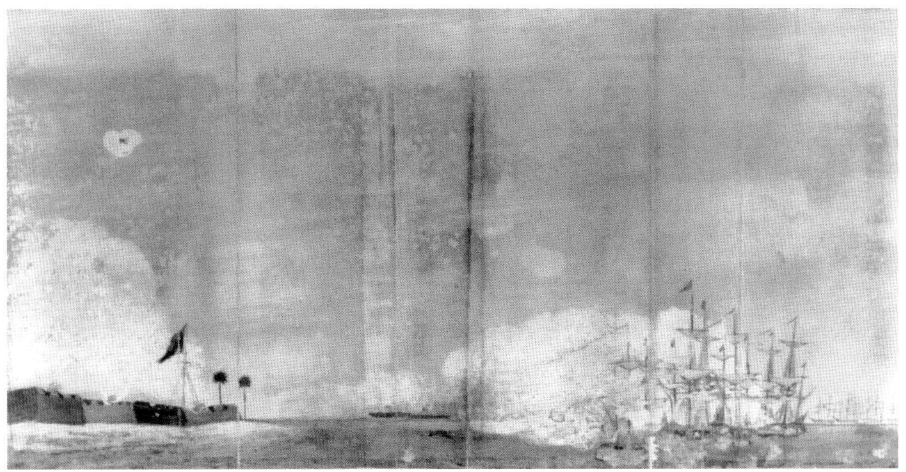

The attack on Fort Sullivan, painted by Henry Gray in 1776. *Courtesy of Library of Congress.*

the morning of June 28, the attack began, but it did not go as planned. The shots of the British warships were completely ineffective on the fort, as its spongy, palmetto-barricaded walls absorbed the blows. While the American fort withstood the blows, the British ships sustained heavy losses from the guns of the fort. Clinton's ground troops fared no better, as American troops stopped them from entering Sullivan's Island.

The British had to destroy one of their ships, and Parker's crew saw more than two hundred sailors either killed or wounded, including Parker himself. Clinton had no choice but to sail back to New York and admit defeat. The South Carolinians had protected Charleston by both the land and sea and rejoiced in their victory. They were thrilled with their success over the mighty British fleet, but the truth was that Clinton's attack was not as organized as it should have been. The South Carolina rebels felt very confident, which would not serve them well the next time the British came to Charleston. Despite the strong feelings of nationalism surging through the Patriots, there were large numbers of Loyalists still supporting the British cause in South Carolina—a problem Greene would have to deal with when he made his way south.

Clinton came back south and initiated attacks on Savannah in the last days of 1778.[17] The British easily took the city and in not too much time had more than four thousand men in Georgia. They took Augusta one month later, and this soon became Major General Benjamin Lincoln's problem as he took over command in South Carolina of the Southern Department, including Virginia, the Carolinas and Georgia. The Americans had been trying to improve the defenses of Charleston and the surrounding area, but the city was still not ready for an attack.

After the defeat at Savannah, the British sailed up to Charleston in May 1780, and Lincoln was faced with an invasion force of ten thousand men. The governor of South Carolina pressured him to defend Charleston rather than surrender to the invaders. Moultrie found the town in absolute chaos, and his soldiers shared the same sentiments. The British were quickly able to surround the city. Consequently, the governor changed his mind and demanded that Lincoln surrender Charleston to the British. The fear that was gripping the city of Charleston got to the governor as he learned of the vast numbers under the British. He all but forced Moultrie to send a flag of truce to the British General Prevost. By doing this, Charleston and its people would not be harmed but rather would be prisoners of war.

Having no option at all, Lincoln surrendered his army of 5,500, half of whom were regulars, on May 12, 1780, rather than let the town go to ruin. It was the worst loss suffered by the Continental army in the war. Surrendering Charleston was terrible for the Americans, as they had just given the British a major port city and ability to bring in more troops and supplies from Britain.

Three months later, a disastrous defeat at Camden, South Carolina, in August 1780 was the second huge loss suffered by the Americans in the South. North Carolinians were desperate for the Continental army to

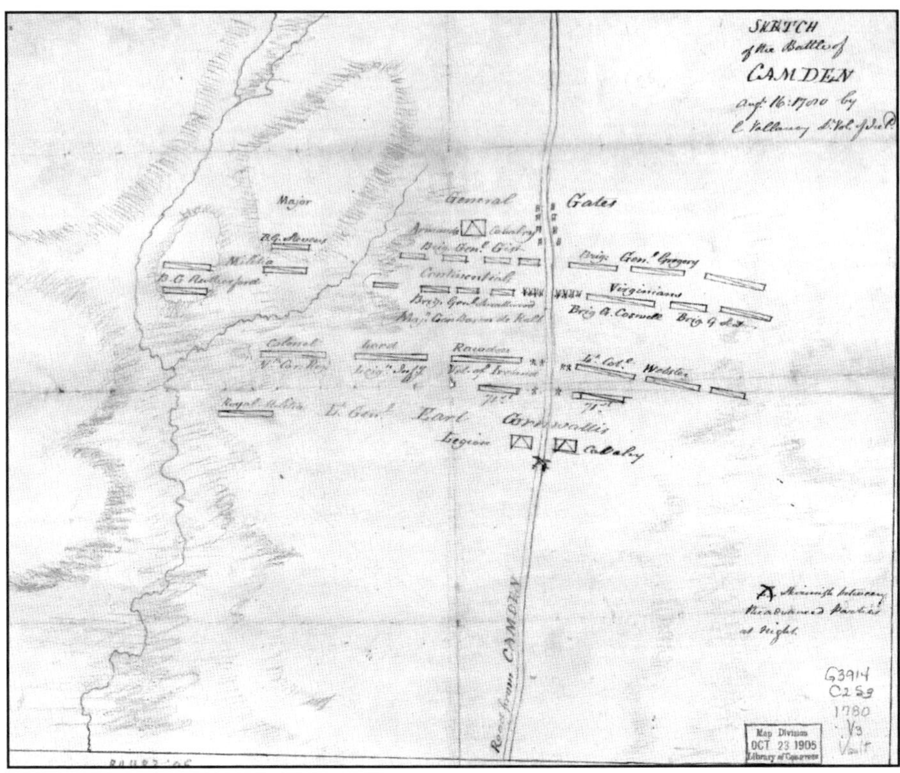

Sketch of the Battle of Camden, August 16, 1780, drawn by Charles Vallancey. *Courtesy of the Library of Congress.*

prevent the British from moving into the state. Gates adjusted his strategy accordingly, but the result was an absolute disaster. His troops were ill-equipped and poorly fed as Gates pushed them through Loyalist country toward Camden. Hostility came not only from the large Tory contingent but also from the land, which did not have anywhere for the troops to forage for food or supplies.

The Americans finally arrived in Camden on the morning of August 16, 1780, to surprise the British army stationed there under Lord Cornwallis. Despite his better judgment, Gates took a gamble and had his weak and starving troops fight the British after the long march. In addition to the questionable decision to push his troops, his military strategy for this engagement was also reckless. He decided to form his entire left flank with militia. The militia used during the Revolutionary War was a military force made up of volunteer civilians to help the American regular army. The use of militia was always a gamble because these men did not have formal

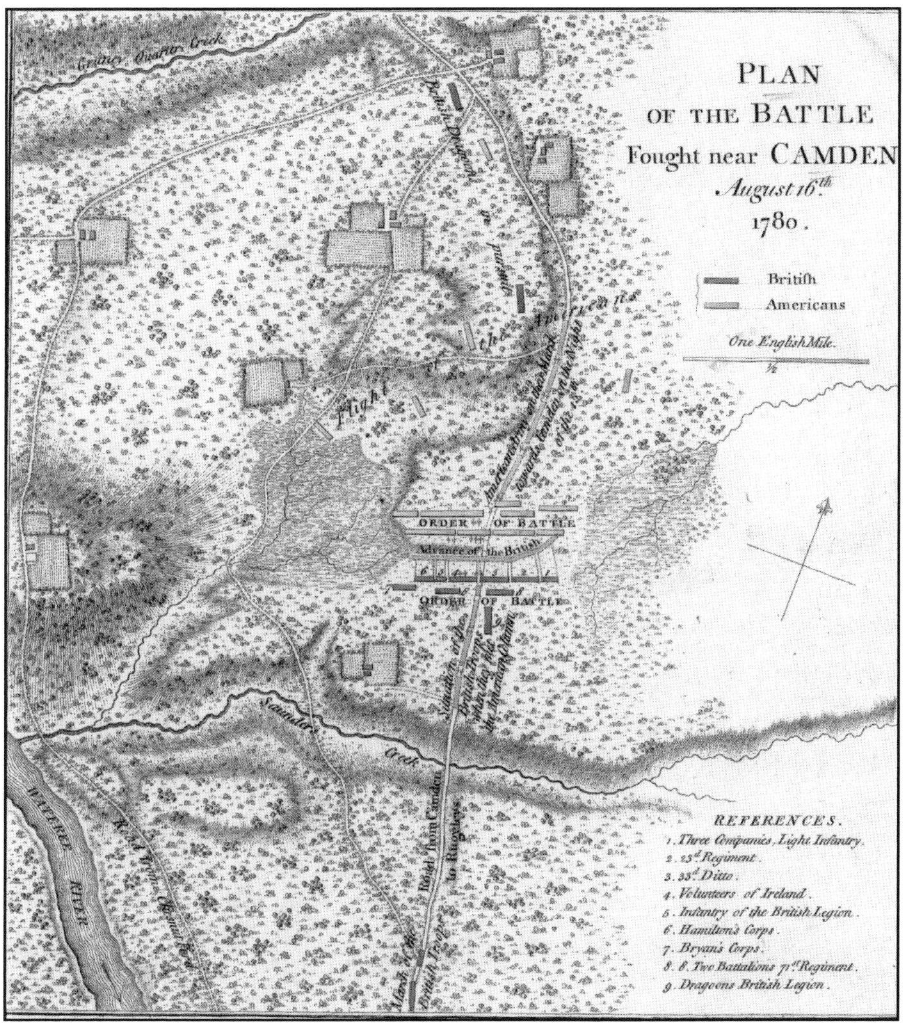

Plan of the Battle of Camden, August 16, 1780, by William Faden. Published in London in 1787. *Courtesy of the Library of Congress.*

training, were not properly equipped and were not contracted full-time soldiers. Military commanders usually felt strongly one way or the other about militia. Some felt that they were a group of free soldiers passionate in the cause. Others felt that they were unreliable and lacked the training necessary to be an effective fighting force against the British.

Unfortunately for Gates, his strategy of using the militia ended disastrously. Conrad remarked, "To ask irregulars to withstand a bayonet charge was unrealistic, to put it mildly. Predictably, the militiamen broke and 'ran like a

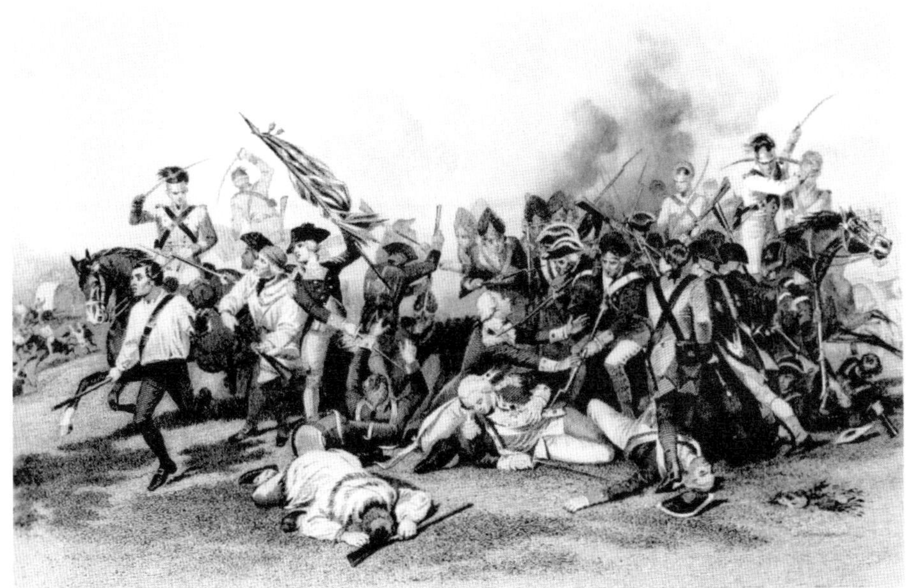

Battle of Camden, death of DeKalb. Engraving from painting by Alonzo Chappel. *Courtesy of the National Archives.*

torrent' without firing a shot when the British first approached."[18] The entire right flank made up of Continentals was completely out in the open and exposed to the British. They fought valiantly, but the sheer number of British soldiers overtook the Americans. Gates brought the rest of his army together after the battle, but only seven hundred regulars were present. It was clear that two significant battles had been lost in the past six months, and politicians felt that it was time for Gates to resign his post immediately.

Horatio Gates was removed, and Greene was called to assume command. Up until this point, the southern campaigns had serious internal issues within the ranks. Historian Dennis Conrad explained, "Military commanders and civilian leaders would often expend as much effort fighting each other as they would contesting the British."[19] This internal feuding is what led to a lack of coordination against the British in Savannah and the subsequent loss of the city to the British in 1779. Benjamin Lincoln wrote to Washington:

> *I found that the army, to use Major General Howe's own words, "has been in a state of abject dependence on the civil authority." Indeed the Continental officer, commanding in this department, had not had it in his power, from the want of supplies which he could control, to march the troops, without the consent of the President of South Carolina, however*

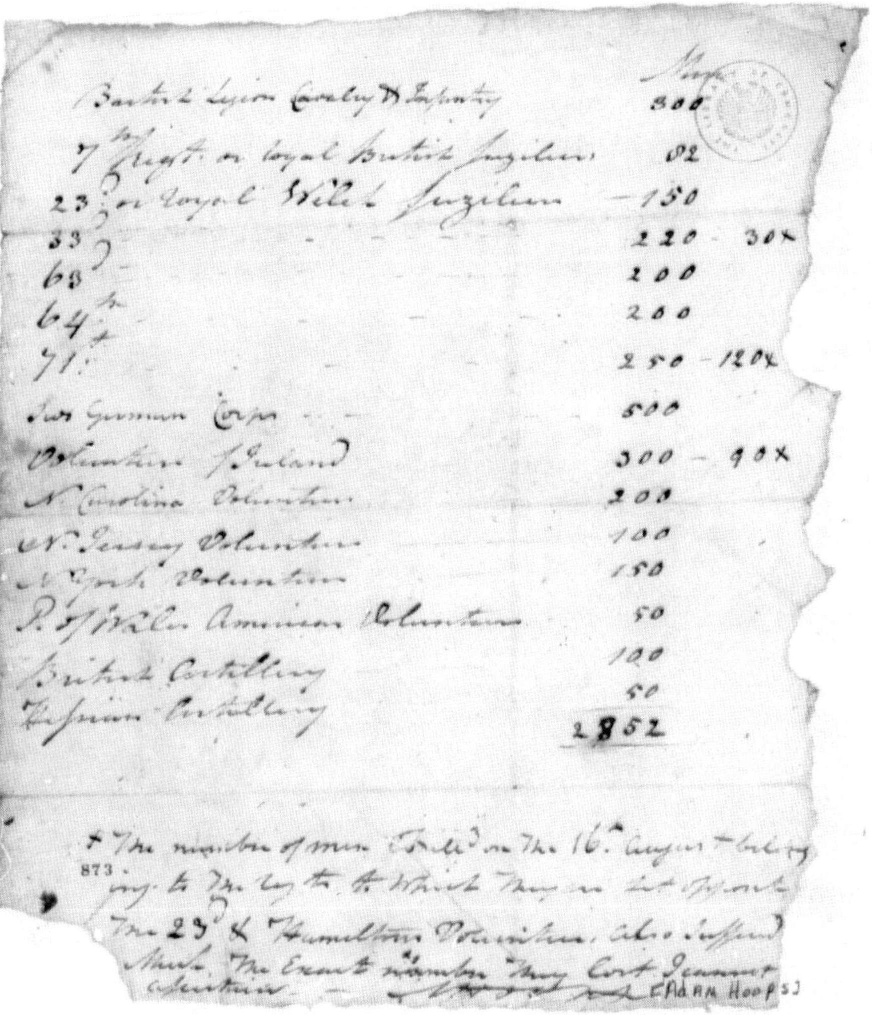

Report on British troop strength at Camden by Major Adam Hoops. *Courtesy of the Library of Congress.*

> *urgent the necessity. I hope things will be better settled, and that I never shall be driven to the hard necessity of altercating with the civil power.*[20]

Unfortunately for Lincoln, this was not the last time he would be dealing with controversy among his own peers. The Siege of Charleston destroyed Lincoln's career just as the Battle of Camden signaled Horatio Gates's end. Political pressure was the downfall of both men in their southern campaigns.

Gates did no better as commander of the South than his predecessor, Lincoln. Washington had thought that Gates would be an excellent choice, as he was known as the hero of Saratoga.[21] Gates was normally an overly cautious general, but this time he took an uncharacteristically daring gamble. He wanted to be the hero who would reverse the damage done in the southern campaigns, but most likely there was some pressure from politicians to make this move just like with Lincoln.

The next general commanding the southern forces would need to be able to take on the British but also handle the fiery local politicians. Greene was the best man for the job given his promising track record. He had great potential as a military strategist on Washington's staff and was deeply interested in politics. This appointment was actually not the first time Greene had been recommended for the position. After Lincoln was captured following the surrender of Charleston, Washington and his friends in Congress suggested Greene. However, the Continental Congress chose Horatio Gates. Its members were dissatisfied with Washington's losing streak and were not about to choose his closest friend as the next commander.

Greene had clashed with Congress before and learned that he would need to be a bit more delicate when working with politicians in the future. Based on his letters, it can be concluded that he was better with the local politicians, but he would still do what he thought best even if it meant disrupting the political process. With Gates's failure, those who had initially supported Washington's suggestion of Greene as the commander of the South gladly put his name forward again and denounced Gates's actions at Camden. There was some controversy, but Greene was the best choice and did receive strong support. It was time for Greene to make something happen and fast. The situation in South Carolina had been disastrous, and being Washington's recommendation, pressure was on Greene to live up to expectations. If Greene failed, the blame would fall on Washington's shoulders. It was up to Nathanael Greene to free Charleston, but it would take him until December 1782 to complete the mission.

Greene had severe problems with lack of supplies and troops in 1782, and this affected his dealings with Loyalists, slaves and civilians. Loyalists were fighting with the British but were mostly defeated by this point save for a few minor skirmishes. Greene tried to entice the Loyalists to come fight for him by promising a pardon if they did. The British were recruiting slaves and Native Americans to take up arms against the Patriots. Greene also wanted to use slaves for his army and suggested granting them their freedom in exchange. The South Carolina government shot down this idea. The British

By the Honourable Nathaniel Greene Esquire, Major General in the Service of the United States, and Commanding Officer of the Southern Department.

To William Christian, William Preston, Arthur Campbell, and Joseph Martin of the State of Virginia, and Robert Sevier, Evan Shelby, Joseph Williams and John Sevier of the State of North Carolina.

Whereas there have arisen Hostilities between the Subjects of the United States Situated on the Western Frontiers of Virginia & North Carolina, and the Nations or Tribes of Indians called the Cherokees, & Chickasaws, from a mutual apprehension of encroachments on the lands of each other. And it being represented to me that a mutual desire hath taken place between the contending parties, to treat on an adjustment of their respective limits, for an exchange of prisoners, a suspension of Hostilities, or conclusion of a peace, which those concerned, Subjects of the United States, conceive they are not at present authorised to enter into. And it being essentially interesting to the service of the Southern Department, that a speedy close be put to the said hostilities: and that harmony between the Contending parties be restored, I do therefore as Commanding Officer of the Southern department hereby nominate and appoint you, the said William Christian

Christian, William Preston, Arthur Campbell, Joseph Martin, Robert Sevier, Evan Shelby, Joseph Williams & John Sevier Esquires, or any five of you, Commissioners on the part of the United States, to meet such Commissioners, as the said Tribes or Nations of Indians shall appoint on their part, at such time & place within the disputed ground as shall be agreed on for the purpose of treating, on the adjustment of the respective limits of each party, an exchange of prisoners, a suspension of Hostilities, conclusion of a peace, or any thing else for the establishment of harmony & good understanding between the contending parties, as to you may seem proper, subject to the confirmation of Congress. In adjusting the limits of the respective parties you are to be governed by the Laws of the said two States of Virginia & North Carolina within their respective Boundaries. You are to exchange such mutual pledges for securing an Observance of the Treaties concluded on, as may be thought necessary, and you are hereby charged to call on the Lieutenants or Commanding Officers of the adjacent Counties within the said two States for force & assistance to prevent any future encroachments by the subjects of the United States on the lands of the said Tribes or Nations of Indians. And as it will contribute much to remove the jealousies now entertained by the

Above, left: Front page of correspondence from Major General Greene to Arthur Campbell appointing him as United States commissioner to the Cherokee and Chickasaw tribes, dated February 26, 1781. *American Revolutionary War Papers of the Charleston Museum Archives.*

Above, right: Second page of correspondence from Major General Greene to Arthur Campbell. *American Revolutionary War Papers of the Charleston Museum Archives.*

Right: Third page of correspondence from Major General Greene to Arthur Campbell. *American Revolutionary War Papers of the Charleston Museum Archives.*

those Tribes of Indians, and the laying a foundation for the establishment of harmony & a good Understanding between the Subjects of the United States & them, to afford the said Tribes of Indians every mark of our good dispositions towards them, you will call on them to appoint certain persons from amongst themselves, to go to Congress for Obtaining such arrangements, or confirmations of their Treaties as may appear to them requisite.

This Commission is to continue in force till revoked, by the Commanding Officer of the Southern department, The Commander in Chief of the American Army, or The Honble the Congress of the United States.

Given Under my hand in Camp in Caswell County North Carolina this twenty sixth day of February one thousand seven hundred & Eighty one

Nath Greene.

had been trying to recruit the slaves of Patriots to fight for their own forces and utilize their knowledge of the land. Despite Greene's best efforts to do the same, South Carolinians wanted to preserve their own way of life and keep their slaves to work the land. Having slaves meant achieving a certain social standing, and fighting alongside slaves was not part of the Patriots' plan. Furthermore, South Carolinians knew that they did not have reason to fear the slaves in the later part of the war because the slaves were fearful of the repercussions if they were caught after fleeing to the British side.[22]

Greene knew the importance of public support, and this greatly influenced his actions between 1780 and 1782. The locals were upset with the army for stealing provisions from their homes, hated the Loyalists and did not want to see them pardoned and viewed the British as weak by arming slaves to fight but did not want to free their own.[23] The war has been described as a civil war conflict between Patriots and Loyalists. Loyalists tried to fight back but had no hope, so they either evacuated South Carolina or fought with the Patriot army to receive a pardon in accordance with one of Greene's postwar plans.

Patriots were seizing the property of Loyalists, and there was nothing they could do about it. Greene hated the practice of impressment but found that it was the only way to gain supplies for his army.[24] He wanted to do this with as much civility as possible, as he wanted the South Carolinians to continue to support the war despite their weariness of the long conflict. Their growing passivity on the matter was fueled by the lack of battles, the appearance of weakness on the side of the British by using slaves and the general feeling that the war was won. The government echoed the sentiments of the public, which is why the war continued to be drawn out, as Greene did not have proper provisions to force the British out until December 1782.

Greene's life would have been quite different than it had been prior to December 1780 if he had never come south. The course of the war would have been much different if Greene had not come south. South Carolina had a series of defeats before Greene took command. For the cause of the American Revolution, it was a good thing Greene came to the rescue when he did.

Chapter 2

"READY AT ALL TIMES TO BLEED IN MY COUNTRY'S CAUSE"

Permit me then to recommend from the sincerity of my heart, ready at all times to bleed in my country's cause, a Declaration of Independence, and call upon the world and the Great God who governs it to witness the necessity, propriety and rectitude thereof.

—Greene to Washington

Greene's letter to Washington categorizes his feelings not only about the Patriot cause but also about what he would give to the effort over the course of the war. When he took over an ineffective fighting force at the end of 1780, Greene's leadership transformed it into an army that forced the British to give up control of the interior of the South and eventually evacuate completely from its shores. Some of the more dramatic moments of the struggle that contributed to the Patriots' later victories were the Battle of Cowpens, the Race to the Dan and Guilford Court House.

While these actions were extremely important in the war in the South, Greene made more contributions than just these engagements. Even though Greene has been named the master strategist of the American Revolution, the bitter truth is that he was not the most daring and imaginative of generals.[25] It was Greene's conservative strategies that led to his success in preserving his regular army to prevent dispersal and defeat. He was very much a disciple of George Washington in his military strategy. They both were highly concerned with preserving the army, using strategic retreat when necessary, engaging the enemy only when victory was possible and even likely, keeping public opinion in mind, exercising moderation toward Loyalists and restoring civil government in the world to come after the war.

Another key to his success was using groups that he greatly disliked in battle: partisan groups and organized militia. These groups helped to harass the British outposts in South Carolina so that the Redcoats could no longer stay camped in and maintain those forts. The single most important aspect in Greene's person that led to his success was his uncommon ability as an organizer.[26] He knew the terrain, he could keep his troops in line and he knew how to efficiently design a logistical system of command. These abilities made Greene successful in the southern campaigns. In his doctoral dissertation, Conrad, editor of *The Papers of General Nathanael Greene*, claimed, "To call him a master strategist would be extreme; it may be contended with greater reason that he was savior of the South."[27]

Greene's most difficult assignment was just beginning. Before receiving the appointment, Nathanael "was preparing for an uneventful winter as commander of the American post at West Point, New York. Such a rest was well deserved."[28] Greene had been serving the war effort since the very beginning. By this time, he was thirty-eight, had worked hard all over the North and had become George Washington's most trusted man and problem solver. Washington had given him many difficult assignments, so he was looking forward to a less stressful post as commander at West Point. Greene's wife was planning to stay with him in the garrison, as she often did. The parties and company of the other military wives was more alluring than a quiet life alone with her children. However, Greene would neither see his wife nor have a restful winter.

Washington had selected this new task for Greene, which would be his hardest yet. He was essentially asked to fix a failed campaign as commander of the Southern Department. Greene was always a man of virtue who answered when duty called, so he accepted. Greene found the situation in the southern states to be dire and lacking any sort of leadership. He arrived in the South and found it to be much different than anything he had yet experienced in the North. Not only was the terrain unfamiliar and difficult, with the number of rivers cutting through the land, but he also had to deal with punishing temperatures and a large number of Loyalists and neutrals.

He stepped into a civil war of sorts between the Patriots and Loyalists in the Carolinas.[29] The civilians and combatants alike were divided on whether to forge a new nation or stay with the British for a number of reasons. Most southern Loyalists' reasoning for siding with Britain had to do with not wanting radical change, fear of chaos and war, lack of confidence in the Patriots and desire for protection of businesses and trade. The Carolinas were perhaps more divided than any other colony.

The problems did not end there for Greene. His army of 2,307 men was weak and badly equipped. Greene knew how desperately important proper supplies were and how they would sometimes decide the battle. Only 1,482 men were fit for duty, with 90 cavalrymen, 60 artillerymen and 949 Continentals. The rest were militia. The number of men who were properly clothed and armed was less than 800.[30] He had to hold together this small and flighty army and prepare it to defeat a mighty British force stationed all over South Carolina.

When Greene assumed command of the Southern Department in December 1780, he found that no records had been kept by Gates. The new general worked immediately to remedy both problems of supplies and morale, much to the pleasure of his peers. However, the lack of clothing proved to be the most desperate and pressing. The South had no capacity to manufacture supplies, as there was not much industry there. Manufactured goods would have to come from the North. Greene requested three to four thousand guns from the northern states, as well as ammunition boxes and medical supplies. His supply demands from Virginia, in particular, were heavy, but he was able to justify his requests. As the former quartermaster, Greene knew how important having proper supplies was, but even his connections could not get him all he needed. Clothing was another story. Greene wrote to Governor Thomas Jefferson in Virginia an angry letter that accused the state of indifference to the well-being of its troops:

> *Your troops may literally be said to be naked. It will answer no good purpose to send men here in such condition, for they are nothing but deadweight. The article of clothing is but a small part of the expense in raising, equipping, and subsisting an army, and yet on this alone the whole benefit of their service depends. The states may seem to deserve credit from having numbers in the field, however wretched their condition, but a general with such troops can give no protection to the country.*[31]

A week after Greene wrote this letter, he was forced to send a Virginia brigade back home with a warning to Jefferson not to send the troops to his command until they had proper clothing. Greene was also upset with Jefferson over how much he and Virginia used the militia. Previous southern leadership relied heavily on the volunteer armies because they often had no choice. Like many

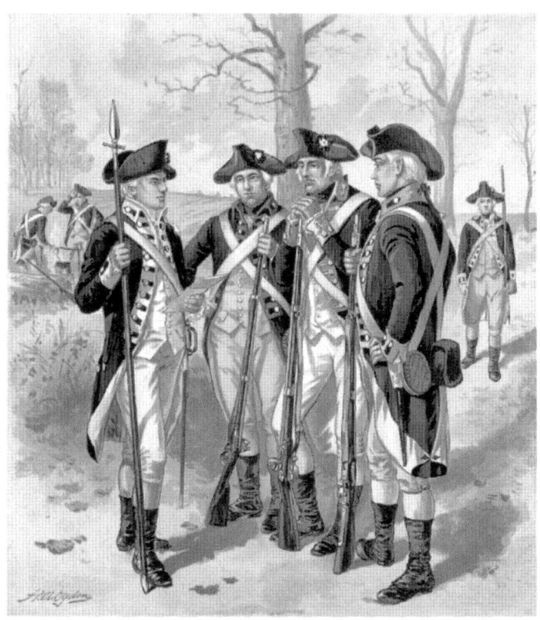

American Continental army, 1779–83. Uniforms and weapons were a luxury not afforded to all American soldiers. Illustration by Henry Alexander Ogden. *Courtesy of Library of Congress.*

Continental officers, Greene did not trust the militia, as the men would often flee at the first sign of trouble.

He felt it compulsory to recruit more troops for the regular army. The Southern Department had also been relying on foreign-born cavalry as dragoons in addition to the militia because it was difficult to recruit for the regular army. Dragoons were a skilled, armed and horse-mounted regiment. Because of this, Greene would use the militia fairly often in months to come, mostly because he had no other option, but he would do so intelligently as part of his overall strategy.

Another major problem that Greene faced upon arrival at camp was the lack of discipline in the troops. The men became addicted to looting and were a danger to the inhabitants of surrounding towns. In addition to the bad habits and misconduct, there was a food shortage, leading to more looting and further bad spirits. Lack of clothing, food and discipline characterized the Southern Army. Greene wrote to Joseph Reed in January 1781, "This army is in such a wretched condition that I hardly know what to do with it. The officers have got such a habit of negligence and the soldiers so loose and disorderly, that it is next to impossible to give it a military complexion."[32]

The men also simply left camp without permission and returned whenever they pleased. Greene was not used to this poor behavior and decided to take harsh action. He threatened to hang anyone who deserted or left without permission. To make himself perfectly clear, Greene immediately seized one of the deserted who had returned and hanged him. The troops felt the ramifications of this action instantly and shaped up enough to be effective in later battles. Figures of desertion in the American Revolution state that one-third of the regulars and half of the militia in Patriot armies deserted, and

South Carolina was not an exception. Greene's threats and punishments definitely contributed to the development of better discipline in the camp. More importantly, Greene instilled in the troops a confidence that he would improve their lot in the war. They became optimistic and almost businesslike as their morale boosted.

A credit to Greene's character was his treatment of Gates's reputation when he arrived, which also boosted morale. It was known that Greene disliked Horatio Gates, and he especially did not appreciate being passed over as commander of the southern campaigns in favor of Gates. Washington had chosen Greene, but Gates was still selected by the Continental Congress. Greene saw Washington as his closest friend and mentor and felt that Gates had tried to discredit him in the past. Greene, however, did not speak ill of his fallen predecessor, treated him with kindness and did not encourage an investigation of Gates's failures. Greene's actions won him respect among the men of the southern command.[33] Another positive was the addition of Lieutenant Colonel Henry Lee's Virginia Legion to the Southern Department. Henry Lee III, or "Light-Horse Harry," commanded a mixed unit of light infantry and dragoons. Having Lee on board would give Greene an excellent fighting force and allow him to create a new strategy for the South.[34]

The first major order of business for Greene was to survey the land and figure out how to get supplies to his army should they be obtained. Washington had suggested utilizing the rivers as a transportation network because wagons were in short supply. Greene thought that this was a good idea and sent out scouting parties to map out the lay of the land. Not only was he able to figure out the river system to move supplies around—although ultimately it seemed that would not be feasible—but he also gathered vital information on the topography. He learned about the condition of the roads, nature of fords and depth of the foliage. Greene was able to understand the terrain and formulate the possibilities for his military. Later on, this knowledge would prove vital in saving the Americans from the British in the "Race to the Dan" in which Greene was greatly praised for his strategy.

When Greene reached South Carolina, he met with John Rutledge, governor of South Carolina, and officially replaced Gates. They spent a considerable amount of time together, as Greene needed to have the support of Rutledge for military and political matters. Having the governor on his side would help him with Congress as he made decisions for the Southern Department.

Greene made the important strategic decision upon arriving in South Carolina to divide his troops. This would set the pattern for all campaigns

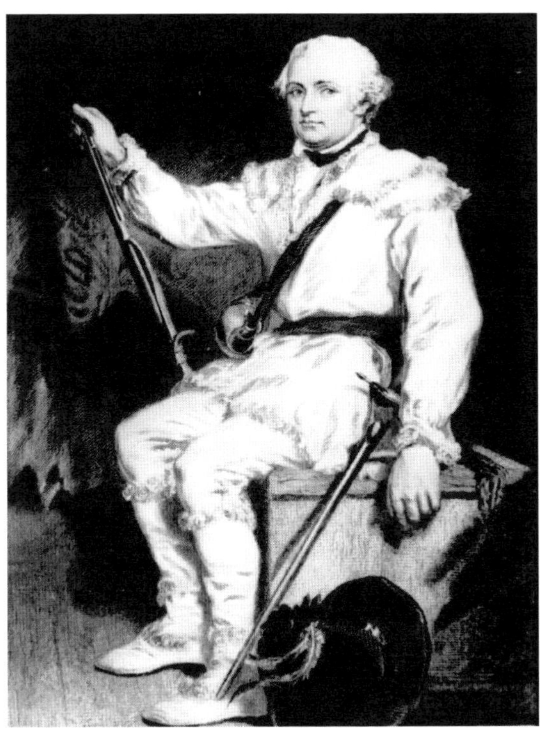

Daniel Morgan. Engraving (full length) from painting by Alonzo Chappel. *Courtesy of the National Archives.*

in the South. This decision was suggested by a number of men who wanted Brigadier General Daniel Morgan to move westward. Greene accepted ideas openly but ultimately made the final call, as he did in all major decisions. Greene was a student of military strategy. Because of this, he understood the dangers of dividing an entire army. Greene had even been part of a divided-army fiasco with his own Patriot troops at the Battle of Long Island.

He ultimately decided to divide the army because this plan would fit his strategy for the South. The army as a whole was not strong enough to face Cornwallis's vast numbers in a traditional battle. Greene thought it best to rely on mobility, with a fast army made up of cavalry and infantry. He felt that cavalry and legion corps were "best adapted to the make of the country and the state of war in that quarter, both for leading and encouraging the inhabitants…by checking and restraining the Depredations of the enemy."[35] The cavalry would be able to confine the British and make it difficult for them to spread throughout the backcountry of South Carolina. The addition of Henry Lee's mounted legion would be integral to this strategy. He wrote to George Washington:

> *This will make the most of my inferior force, for it compels my advisory to divide his, and holds him in doubt as to his own line of conduct. He cannot leave Morgan behind him to come at me, or his posts at Ninety-Six and Augusta would be exposed; and he cannot chase Morgan far or prosecute his views in Virginia while I am here with the whole country before me.*[36]

Washington would write back and warn him of the vast rivers in central South Carolina, which would make maneuvering around swampy Charleston difficult. Greene hoped to win most battles in the upcountry to avoid moving too close to the British-occupied city of Charleston.

Greene wanted Morgan's detachment to harass the British stationed at Ninety-Six. That would include disrupting their supply lines and being ready to join Greene's main body if Cornwallis positioned for battle in the northwestern part of the state. Greene needed to make a big call like this to restore American dominance and boost morale.

Cornwallis was initially puzzled by Greene's strategy to divide his troops. This decision, coupled with Cornwallis's lack of military intelligence, forced him to divide his own men in response, which created the possibility for the two forces to meet in different places. The success of Greene's tactical genius was demonstrated in January 1781 at the Battle of Cowpens, which was a major victory for the Patriots under Nathanael Greene's command. Much success was owed to the militia, which Greene ironically disliked. This encounter was the pivotal battle of the war in the South. As Conrad explained, "Although the numbers of men engaged were not impressive, the combined total of the two armies involved only 2,000 men, the reaction of the two commanders to the actions of their subordinates on the field at Cowpens did indeed have far-reaching results in this last British campaign for the subjugation of America."[37] Greene had assigned one thousand of his men to Morgan, a tactical genius like Greene, who was able to crush Colonel Banastre Tarleton at the Battle of Cowpens.

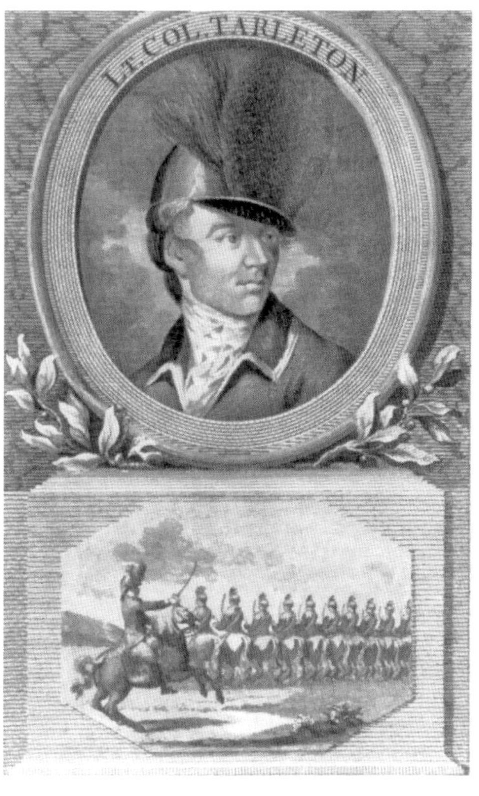

Lieutenant Colonel Tarleton, published by J. Walker, April 1, 1782. *Courtesy of Library of Congress.*

It did not look like Morgan was going to beat the British this time,

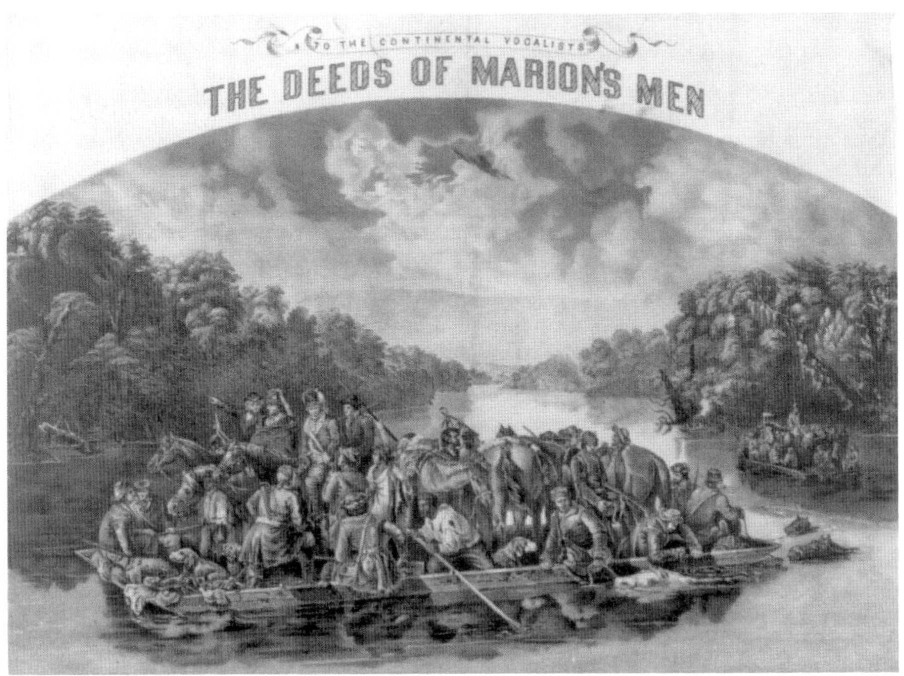

Francis Marion and his men crossing the Pee Dee River in South Carolina. Published by Russell & Tolman in 1860, lithograph by James G. Clark. *Courtesy of Library of Congress.*

though, and there was not supposed to be a battle at all. Tarleton's mission was to be supporting the British post at Ninety-Six, but his men skirmished with some of Morgan's men in the nearby area. Tarleton commanded a British legion of dragoons. Tarleton thought it was Morgan and the Americans' objective to attack the British at their western forts in South Carolina.[38] He traveled to Ninety-Six but found no danger. Actually, Colonel Francis Marion was only a few miles away, and he would create a threat. Marion, the "Swamp Fox," was a gifted leader of the irregular South Carolina militia. Tarleton remarked that Marion's guerrilla warfare style of fighting made him difficult to catch, as he and his men hid in the swamps of the Lowcountry and attacked at random. It was Tarleton himself who gave Marion this famous nickname.

After surveying the land around Ninety-Six, Tarleton decided that it was time to make a move; he would be the one to find Morgan's army and cut off its escape route if it should move back to Greene's command. He appealed to Cornwallis for men and permission to pursue Morgan and received both. He had heard that Morgan was being reinforced by a huge number of militia, so he made it possible for Leslie and Cornwallis's men to join together to pursue the Americans. With a series of quick marches toward Morgan, Tarleton finally caught up, trapping the Americans between the rising Broad River and more than one thousand British troops. Morgan knew that he was penned and needed to face the British or surrender.[39]

Whether Morgan purposely chose this spot for battle, as he later contended, or Tarleton forced him to fight on this disadvantageous ground is still a matter of historical debate. Cowpens is exactly the type of ground the British wanted when battling Americans, so why would Morgan choose this spot as he said? Tarleton reported:

> *The ground was disadvantageous for the Americans, and convenient for the British. An open wood was certainly as good a place for action as Lieutenant Colonel Tarleton could desire; America does not produce many more suitable to the nature of the troops under his command.*[40]

This battlefield was a long and open plain that slopped upward to a ridge spotted with trees that worked well for cavalry needing wide-open spaces to ride. The Broad River behind Morgan prevented any retreat for the Americans, who were outnumbered three to one on horsemen. Conditions seemed ideal for a massive British victory and less than ideal for Morgan, who was later adamant that he chose the site himself and was not forced into it. He claimed that he chose Cowpens because he understood the power but also fickleness of the militia and knew how to use it. He did not want to cross the Broad River because he feared that his militia would desert, as part-time soldiers often did. Having the river behind their flanks would deny the militiamen the ability to flee. The irony is that two-thirds of Morgan's army was militia; he would have to rely heavily on that force that he trusted so little.

Despite this bleak outlook, the Americans were able to win and win big, destroying 90 percent of Tarleton's command while only losing 25 of their own men.[41] This success was due mostly to Morgan's battle plan. While the militia was not always the most reliable, its main talent was marksmanship. The front line was made of 150 riflemen who were sharpshooters, whose mission was to slow the British advancing lines. After firing a few rounds, they were to retreat, and the second line, which was also composed of militia under Andrew Pickens, advanced forward. They were to continue the work of the first line by firing off two rounds when the British got close enough. Militia was useless when it came to withstanding a bayonet charge, so Morgan planned for them to retreat after firing. He was rather daring in his strategic use of the militia by using the least reliable of his men in such

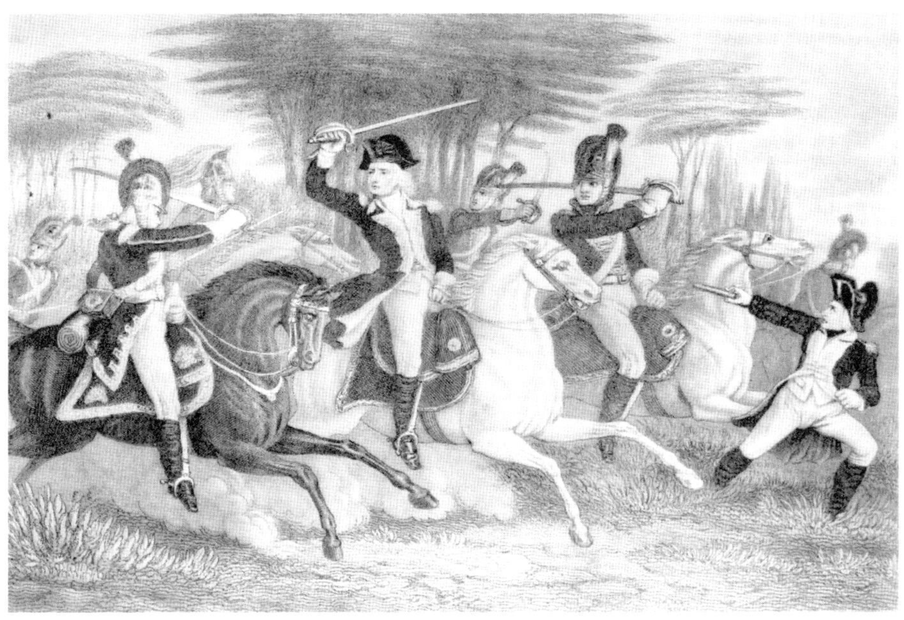

Colonel William Augustine Washington at the Battle of Cowpens. Drawn and engraved for *Graham's Magazine* by S.H. Gimber. *Courtesy of the National Archives.*

a way. The third line was on higher ground and made up of Morgan's best men, his most seasoned veterans ready to pick up where the militia left off. Morgan encouraged his men by telling them that he had confidence in them and that they only needed to do their part to achieve victory.[12]

Tarleton and his men arrived on the field at 8:00 a.m. on that cold January 16, 1781 morning and quickly deployed his troops after surveying the Americans' position. His troops did not have time to rest after their long march, and Tarleton did not confer with his officers to make a battle plan. His battle lines and dragoons ran right into Morgan's snipers, and the Redcoats answered with a bayonet charge. The militia retreated as expected but lured the British into the American horsemen, who rode with a vengeance. A misunderstanding occurred when some of the militia retreated and other officers thought that an entire retreat had been called. They ordered their men to retreat over the hill.

The British thought the battle was won, but Morgan took advantage of the confusion and had his men re-form and start a bayonet charge. This charge, coupled with the American dragoons and sharpshooters, overcame the British lines. Tarleton was chased from the field. Some of his horsemen, artillery and 889 foot soldiers were captured. About 90 percent of Tarleton's command was killed or captured at Cowpens, and his supply train was cut off. The Americans only lost 12 men killed and 60 wounded. This battle was a critical turning point in the war in that from this point on, Cornwallis made a series of tactical errors leading up to Yorktown. Each mistake can all be traced to this battle and to Greene and Morgan's strategy in their victory at Cowpens.

Despite celebrations and a feeling that all was won in the South because of the Battle of Cowpens, Greene remained concerned about the situation of the American army. This was a personality trait of his; Greene was always pessimistic even in victory, anticipating what was to come and preparing for anything. He was a careful and conscientious commander, and this way of thinking would serve him well in the coming months. Upon hearing of the great victory, he wrote to Francis Marion, "After this nothing will appear difficult."[43] After thinking more about the situation, Greene added, quite in character:

> *This is a great affair were our situation such as to take proper advantage of it; but for want of that, I fear little good will result from it, as to the final victory of this country. The situation of these States is wretched, and the distress of the Inhabitants exceeds all description; nor is the condition of the enemy more agreeable. We have but few troops fit for duty, and all those are employed upon difficult attachments, the success of which depend upon time and chance.*[44]

Greene was always worried about the condition of his army and the desperate need for supplies. He regretted that boasting and exaggerated tales of Morgan's success would stop Congress and the state governments from sending aid and relief. Greene realized that he was not going to get what he needed, so he decided to bring the two wings of his army back together and organize a retreat back to North Carolina. Plunging farther into South Carolina would be too risky.

Chapter 3

"RISE AND FIGHT AGAIN"

We fight, get beat, rise, and fight again.
—Greene on the "Race to the Dan"

In preparation for the planned retreat, Greene told Marion to begin a series of attacks on British supply lines to encourage resistance and distract the British. Next, he gave main control of his army to his second in command, Isaac Huger, and told him to march north to meet up with the rest of the army. Greene had his own mission to attend to, and on January 28, 1781, with just three men, he traveled 120 miles through enemy territory to reach Morgan. A risky move indeed, but Greene had heard that Morgan wished to retire soon, and he needed not only to gain control of his men but also discuss strategy at a very important point in the war before Morgan did anything drastic. With Greene's men retreating north, he did not want Morgan and his men to isolate themselves from the rest of the Southern Army. Luckily, Greene's ride was successful, and he arrived at Morgan's camp on the Catawba River.

Meanwhile, Cornwallis learned of the dreadful defeat at Cowpens from Tarleton and resolved to free his prisoners held by the Americans. However, he made a few mistakes that would allow the Americans to get away and go north. Cornwallis marched his men toward Kings Mountain, thinking that the Americans would be confident and try to gain more ground toward the interior of South Carolina. He figured that they would hold their ground at least and then march on to the fort at Ninety-Six, near present-day Greenwood. Morgan, however, was already retreating in the opposite direction, and Cornwallis did not learn of this until later, when Morgan was already across two rivers. Cornwallis ordered his men to do whatever it took to catch up, but that included burning his own supplies and deteriorating his army. The British chased Morgan out of South Carolina and eventually all the way up to the Virginia border a month later. Greene joined in and had not originally intended to march all the way north, but he thought that this would surprise the British and wear them down in a chase.

This retreat turned into a series of skirmishes in which Greene gradually wore down the British. These military engagements are known as the "Race to the Dan" because the Dan River flows in northern North Carolina and that is where the encounters were leading. The skirmishes eventually culminated in the Battle of Guilford Court House, located near present-day Greensboro, on March 15, when Greene felt strong enough to face Cornwallis directly. Greene had been worried about getting enough militiamen to join with his regular Continentals during his retreat.

Luckily, as his army crossed the Dan River on February 14, Greene received word that large numbers of militia were in Virginia and eastern North Carolina waiting for a mission. They were not able to keep up with the speed of Greene's retreat to join. Through the retreat, he lost many militiamen as they deserted and returned home. Greene had hoped that he would gain more men for the impending conflict, but he could rest the troops he did have for now, knowing that he had won the Race to the Dan. This planned retreat was a great testament to Greene's military mastermind.

Greene had fewer than 1,600 men. The mission was clear: his army needed to harass the British, overcome the Loyalists and encourage Patriot fervor throughout the area. Greene hoped that he would be able to avoid going into battle with the British, as he mostly had in the Race to the Dan. What Greene did not know was that Cornwallis was having supply issues also and did not have proper intelligence as to the strength of the American army in the area. Cornwallis was concerned that the Americans could isolate his army and hold their ground in North Carolina, as he did not want to retreat back into South Carolina. Cornwallis wanted to take advantage of Loyalist numbers in North Carolina, and to fall back would be to abandon this potential force and admit defeat.

To protect their pride, the British marched to Hillsborough and put out the call to invite all loyal subjects to fight with them under the last royal governor of North Carolina.[15] Initially, a huge number of Loyalists turned out, and nine militia companies were formed from the volunteers.

However, just as suddenly, these Tories got scared when they learned that the Americans were in the area, and they felt that the British powers were not concentrated enough to be able to protect them. The Loyalists had had their spirits broken in the past, and they would never be a strong and reliable force for Cornwallis again, a fact that angered and discouraged him.

The last straw that dissuaded any Loyalists from joining with the British was Pyle's Massacre. On February 24, 1781, Colonel John Pyle, commander of the Loyalist militia, and 350 Loyalists from central North Carolina were victims of the combined forces of Colonel Harry Lee and Colonel Andrew Pickens. The Americans had been sent by Greene to monitor British activities, and they learned that Tarleton was nearby. The two set up a hidden camp near the British base of Hillsborough and were able to catch and interrogate two British staff officers and two of Pyle's men to gain further intelligence.

Lee met up with Colonel Pyle to shake hands and exchange the usual civilities before the battle began, which was customary for this time. Lee's Legion of cavalry and Pickens's riflemen destroyed the Loyalist militia as it broke and ran. However, for the entire battle, the Loyalists thought the encounter was a dreadful mistake. They mistook the green uniforms of Lee's Legion for Tarleton's dragoons. The Loyalist militia shouted that they supported King George as the Patriots were cutting them down.[16] Lee and Pickens reveled in their success over the Loyalist militia of John Pyle, who, according to legend, was badly wounded and crawled to a nearby pond to be rescued. The pond is still called Pyle's Pond and is in present-day Alamance County, North Carolina. Lee wrote of the conflict, "The capricious goddess gave us Pyle and saved Tarleton."[17] Tarleton had gotten away, but morale among the Americans was up and morale among the Loyalists and British was down. Loyalist militiamen were not joining the British camp, but Patriot militiamen were joining Greene and the Americans. This switch in militia support would come just in time for another major battle at Guilford Court House.

Nathanael Greene finally got the troops that he was waiting for in March 1781. Continentals and militia numbering about three thousand arrived in the American camp. Greene marched within twelve miles of the British camp in Hillsborough to let Cornwallis know that it was time to face each other after weeks of skirmishes and chases. Cornwallis was up to the challenge, as he knew he could not hold his ground much longer with food stores depleting.

On the morning of March 15, the British marched the twelve miles to Guilford Court House, where Greene and his camp were waiting. Greene had the luxury of choosing the battleground this time, and he made

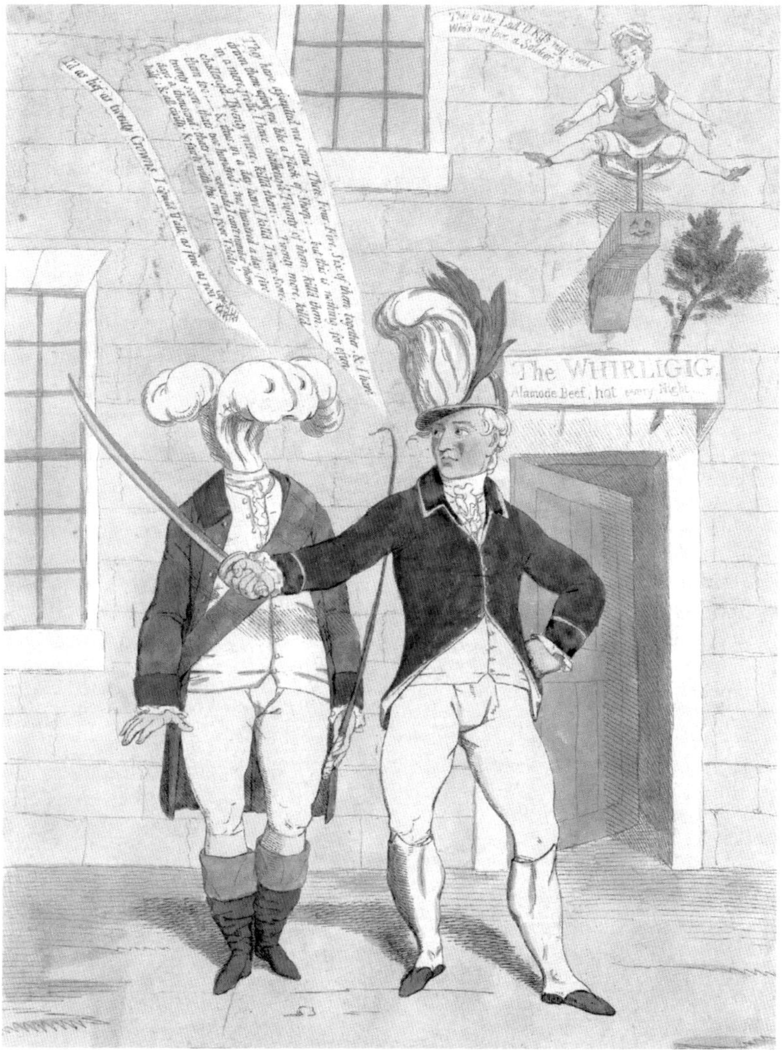

"The Thunderer," Banastre Tarleton, boasts of his exploits to the Prince of Wales. Cartoon printed in 1782 by E.H. D'Achery, St. James Street, *Courtesy of Library of Congress.*

sure to take advantage of that fact. He wished this time to avoid fighting in formations and instead engage the British by taking advantage of the terrain. The grounds had sloping inclines, densely wooded areas, open fields and roads cutting through the middle.

Greene met with his officers and planned to separate his force into three groups to face the British. Militia would once again make up the first line in this battle, just as at Cowpens, and they were to fire three rounds and then retreat. Their marksmanship was the militia's strongest asset, so Greene made sure to capitalize on that with a few well-aimed shots taken first. Lee's Legion and William Washington's cavalry protected both sides, and the Continentals were behind the militia. Greene was determined to preserve his army, which may explain why he would never win a major battle. But in all of Greene's defeats, he still won strategically and forced the British closer to Charleston.

The British arrived at Guilford Court House in the afternoon after marching all morning and had little time to rest before the battle commenced. Greene had 4,400 men against Cornwallis's 1,900.[48] The cannons boomed back and forth as Cornwallis arranged his lines. Tarleton's dragoons remained close by so to be ready when needed. The British began their advance, and the cannons spooked the American militia, who barely fired at all. They broke and ran, causing major problems for Greene. He wrote to Daniel Morgan about the affair, "Had the North Carolina militia done their duty, the victory would have been certain and easy. But, they deserted the most advantageous post I ever saw, without firing a gun."[49]

Lee and the other officers felt the same way as Greene. With the militia gone, the British advanced, and the American groups fired and separated. Three isolated fights broke out as the terrain of rivers, woods and ravines split the armies. The Continentals and cavalry fought bravely, withstanding bayonet attacks and more. However, the British cavalry burst out of the woods and started attacking a newly formed regiment of Continental regulars, and they panicked and ran. This left the American artillery abandoned, and the British captured it, leaving more of the American forces vulnerable. A wild bout of hand-to-hand combat broke out, and Cornwallis could see that the Americans were winning, so he desperately called for the cannons to be loaded. This action would kill both the Americans and his own men, but he felt he had no other option.

After the cannon fire, the British advanced and looked as if they would surround the Continentals. Greene ordered a retreat to save his men from capture, but he had to leave his artillery because the horses had been killed who were pulling them. They retreated ten miles back to their old camp to avoid being pursued by Cornwallis, who claimed the field and victory.

Throughout the entire Race to the Dan and Battle of Guilford Court House, Greene could not say that he won. While each encounter was technically a British victory, they gained no advantage strategically; Cornwallis lost about two thousand men. He was in no position at all to take the offensive again.

The Americans who had lost the day did not feel defeated. Instead, they felt hopeful, knowing that they had done serious damage to the British. Greene had preserved his own army, which was crucial. However, he placed a lot of the blame for the loss on the militia.

While he was disappointed in the men's fleeing the field, he most likely had an agenda for writing to everyone telling them of the militia's failure. Greene had suggested before that the militia be trained as regular Continentals and hoped that putting the blame on the North Carolina militia would encourage the North Carolina Board of War to help him out. Well, as it turned out, Greene was successful, as the board decreed that all militia who fled Guilford Court House were to train in the Continental army for a year. The strategic victory for Greene was much more important than the tactical defeat. Greene perhaps could have won the battle, but it was wiser to preserve the army and retreat, for much was yet to come.

Cornwallis remained on the field for two days following his victory but could not hold the ground with his army in ruin. Fearing another engagement with Greene, Cornwallis was forced to retreat to Wilmington, North Carolina, for supplies, leaving his wounded behind. He was upset he was not able to finish off Greene and his army, but he realized that the vast majority of supplies that Greene was receiving was coming from Virginia.

Up until this point, Virginia had mostly remained untouched by the war. Cornwallis decided that he would invade Virginia to cut off the supply lines running from there to the Carolinas and thus end American resistance there. What he did not know was that he would reach his eventual defeat at Yorktown in the months to come.

Greene decided against chasing him back to Virginia and decided to return to South Carolina, which was now open for him to "begin a campaign to recapture the British stronghold in the South."[50] This decision was a bold move for Greene, and he knew the strategy was a gamble. Throughout his effort, Greene achieved strategic success by maintaining his Continental army in the field as a consistent threat to the British garrisons. He justified himself to many, writing a number of letters. He felt that "[t]he boldness of the maneuver will make them think I have secret reasons which they cannot comprehend. If I can get some supplies and secure a retreat, I fear no bad consequences."[51] Greene had begun his re-conquest of South Carolina, but it was not without difficulty.

Lieutenant Colonel Francis Rawdon was the British commander in South Carolina, stationed in Camden. He worried about Greene's men roaming around attacking British posts and for good reason. American Patriots,

Brigadier General Thomas Sumter, Marion and others engaged with the British twenty-six times, taking posts, harassing supply lines, capturing reinforcements and wearing down Rawdon's men throughout the spring. Sumter led the Second South Carolina Regiment and became known as the "Fighting Gamecock" because of his fighting techniques. Banastre Tarleton apparently liked giving nicknames because this one was courtesy of him, as was Marion's "Swamp Fox."

Greene had cut off Rawdon's communications and supplies and hoped to completely isolate Camden by capturing Fort Watson. Lee and Marion joined together on April 14 to form a deadly combination of Continental cavalry and partisan leadership. They surrounded Fort Watson the next day and began their siege, which was not an easy task. The post was on top of a mound about forty feet high and protected by British regulars and Loyalists. Fort Watson was important strategically because it was a major link between Camden and Charleston. If the Americans could take the fort, their operations in the area would be uncontested by the British, and they could cut off British supplies and reinforcements from Charleston. Sumter could surround and isolate Rawdon and his men, and Greene would take Camden. Greene believed in this plan and had Lee and Marion begin the siege.

They started by attempting to cut off the water supply to Fort Watson, but the British commander put a stop to that. Lee requested additional ammunitions and cannons to fire on the post, hoping it would be a quick operation. Greene did not want to risk an extensive engagement without the cannons but ultimately approved and sent provisions to Lee.

One of Marion's officers came up with a plan to take Fort Watson. He suggested a movable tower made of logs that would protect sharpshooters but allow them to fire into the fort. It was constructed and reached almost forty feet tall. On the morning of April 23, 1781, the tower was in position, and the riflemen shot right inside, which kept the British unable to protect the fort from the Patriots bringing down the walls. The British, unable to defend the fort, were forced to surrender the post. Marion and Lee were finally able to replenish ammunitions. The Americans had a key position in between Charleston and Camden and could monitor British operations in the area. Greene was free to try to recapture Camden and make up for the terrible loss there by Gates in August 1780.

Camden was situated on a slight elevation, and Greene chose to encamp his men a mile and a half from Camden at a place called Hobkirk's Hill. Greene did not have enough men to face Rawdon in Camden, so he was hoping he could draw him out to that area, where he had the high ground. A

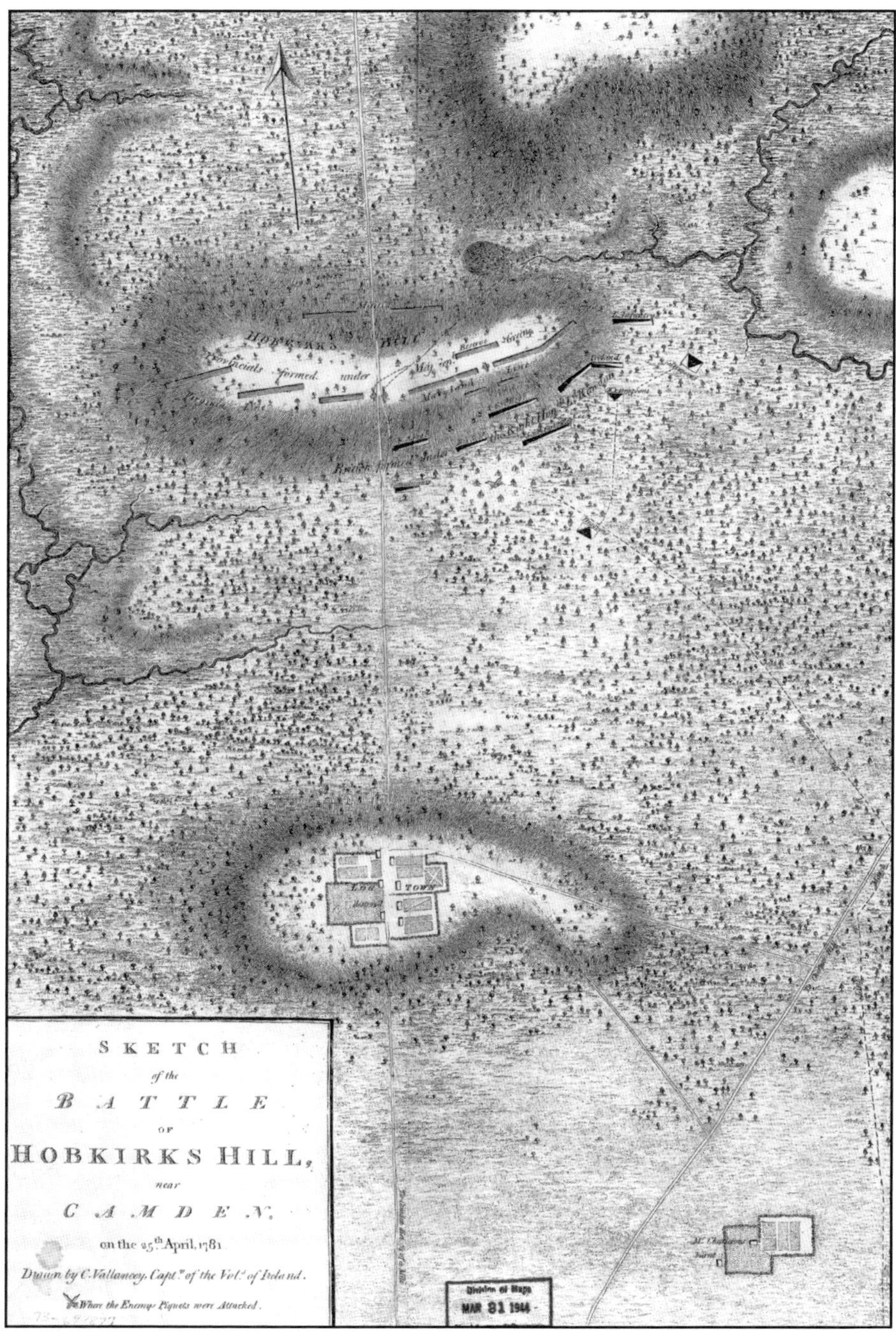

Sketch of the Battle of Hobkirk's Hill, near Camden, on April 25, 1781. Drawn by Charles Vallancey. *Courtesy of the Library of Congress.*

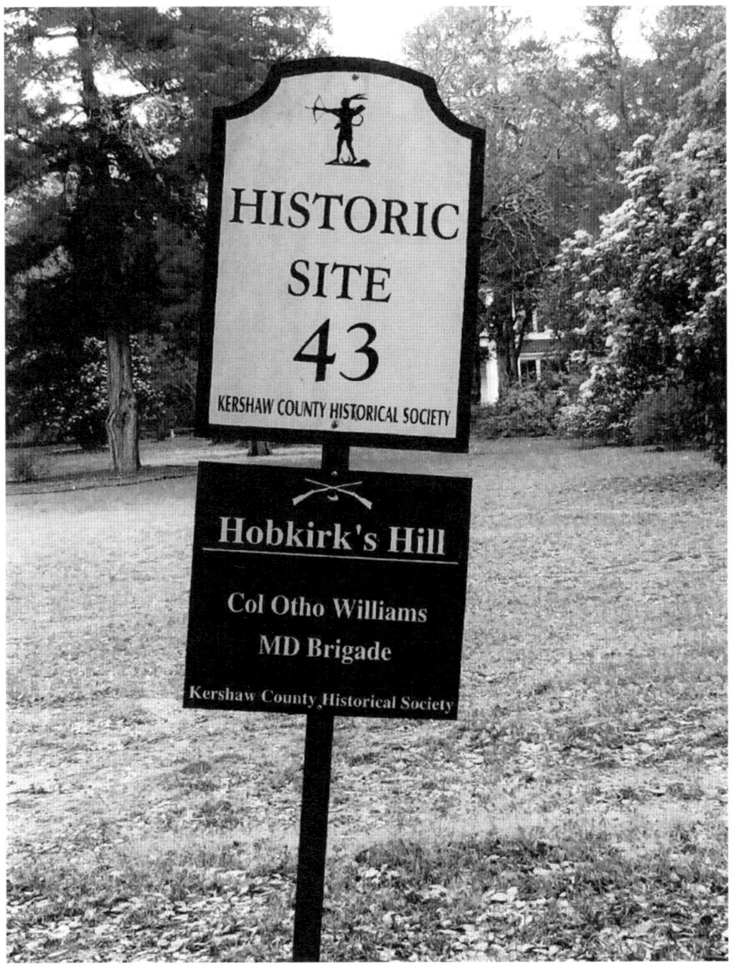

Historic marker outside Camden, South Carolina, of location of Otho Williams's brigade during the Battle of Hobkirk Hill. *Photo by Callie Neal.*

Continental deserter went to Camden and was captured and brought to the British commander. He told of Greene's position, his lack of artillery and the location of various Patriot detachments. Having this new intelligence and news of Fort Watson, Rawdon did take a gamble. On the morning of April 25, he marched out of Camden to meet Greene.[52]

Luckily for Greene, his artillery had just returned that morning, and the Continentals had what they needed to fight. However, the Americans were caught unaware when the British arrived and were occupied with cleaning clothes and cooking. Their advanced picket notified the Patriot forces and

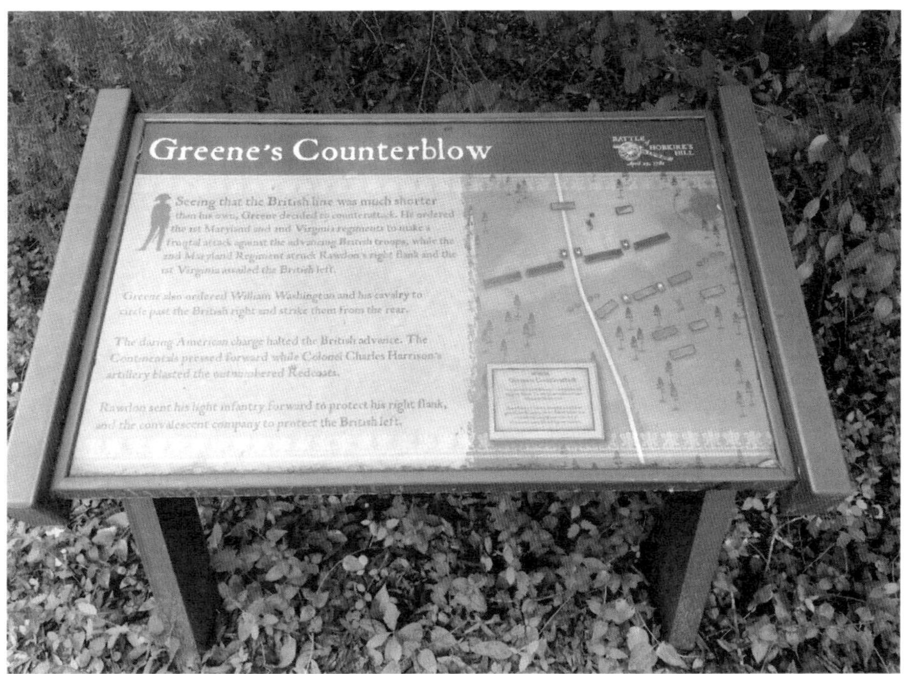

Historic marker at the site of the Battle of Hobkirk's Hill in Camden, South Carolina. Depicts military operations of Greene. *Photo by Callie Neal.*

was able to slow the British enough to give Greene time to issue a battle plan and arrange his lines. He placed his Continentals strategically with the militia behind this time. Dragoons would charge behind the enemy to cut off the escape route to Camden. Greene had brought three cannons ready to fire on the British. Much to Rawdon's dismay, he had none to return fire. They were at the mercy of Greene's artillery, followed by bayonet-charging Continentals. A captain commanding a group of Maryland Continentals was killed, leaving the regiment disorganized. The British took advantage of this and countered with a bayonet charge of their own. Disorder spread, and soon more Continentals fled; Greene had no choice but to call a retreat from Hobkirk's Hill.

This battle was significant for several reasons but primarily because it showed the transition of the nature of fighting in South Carolina and the entire South. Greene, a strategic mastermind, was showing the British how important strategy was in these battles. They began to copy Greene and Morgan's strategy of using the militia to their advantage instead of just part of the regular infantry. Rawdon used his Tory marksmen to his

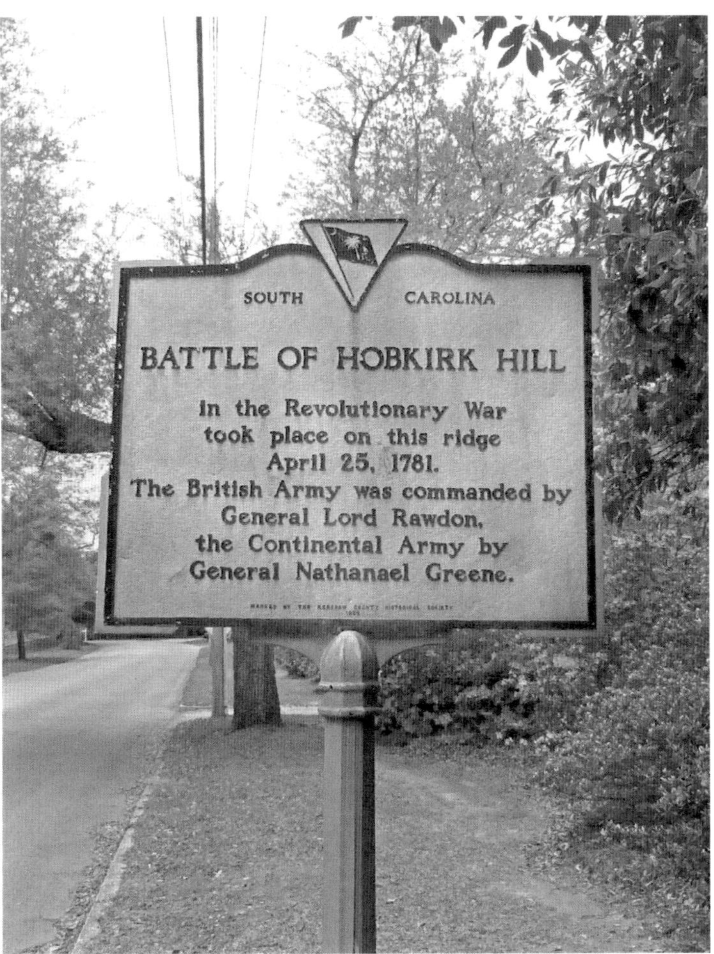

Historic marker at the site of the Battle of Hobkirk's Hill in Camden, South Carolina. Notes basic information about the conflict. *Photo by Callie Neal.*

advantage this time and told them to aim for the American officers to create confusion. The British did exactly this at Hobkirk's Hill.

A fierce clash with small numbers, the Battle of Hobkirk's Hill ended in Rawdon's favor, with Greene retreating miles away. The retreat did not last long, however, for Greene returned to the battlefield, and Rawdon withdrew to Camden. Once again, this was another tactical loss for Greene but a strategic gain. The British commanders were rejoicing in their victory and thought that this would prevent Greene from marching into Charleston and taking back the South. However, they had lost a lot of men, with no hope to replace them.

Greene lost about the same number of men but could gather more militia men in the area. Although he did not trust the militia, the guerrilla warfare was effective.[53] Greene was still seriously lacking trained Continentals, though, and could only muster a few small operations against British posts, while the bulk of the army occupied Rawdon's force in Camden. But Greene and his army "were further advanced into South Carolina than ever before."[54]

A few weeks later, in early May, Rawdon realized he could not stay in central South Carolina due to Greene's presence on one side, General Sumter on the other and Marion thrashing his supply lines and communication with Charleston. Cornwallis was not planning on returning to South Carolina and instead moved into Virginia. Greene wondered what he should do next. He accepted that the role of the Americans in South Carolina would need to turn to attacking the remaining garrisons in the interior so they could control the entire state, save for Charleston. Greene debated leaving South Carolina himself and delegating command to Marion and Sumter. He thought the commander of the Southern Department should be facing the commander of the enemy. Lee advised strongly against this strategy, believing that Marion and Sumter were not adequate replacements for Greene and that the British were still very much a threat in South Carolina. Greene agreed with Lee and turned his attention to dispelling the remaining British from their posts. He would let Cornwallis retreat north, while the bulk of the British army retreated to Charleston.

The first action would be to eliminate a nearby post that the British used as a principal stop for their supply and communications line from Charleston to Camden. The post was actually the plantation home of Rebecca Brewton Motte, the widow of a Patriot, and called Fort Motte. Marion and Lee arrived on May 6 and knew that it needed to be destroyed before Rawdon got there. The mansion had been turned into a formidable fort, with a ditch surrounding the house and 140 men stationed there. However, the Americans had the upper hand with artillery and cannons, while the British had none.

On May 10, 1781, the Patriots were close enough to demand surrender, but the British held on to hope as Rawdon's forces could be seen in the distance. Time was of the essence. Marion and Lee discussed burning down the house in a hurry to get rid of the British. They hesitated because Rebecca Motte would lose her property, and she was a popular Patriot. Legend has it that Mrs. Motte had taken up residence with her children just outside the property and appeared with a bow and arrow to speak with the officers. She did not hesitate for a minute to suggest burning her home and using flaming arrows to do so. She famously told them, "If it were a palace, it should go."

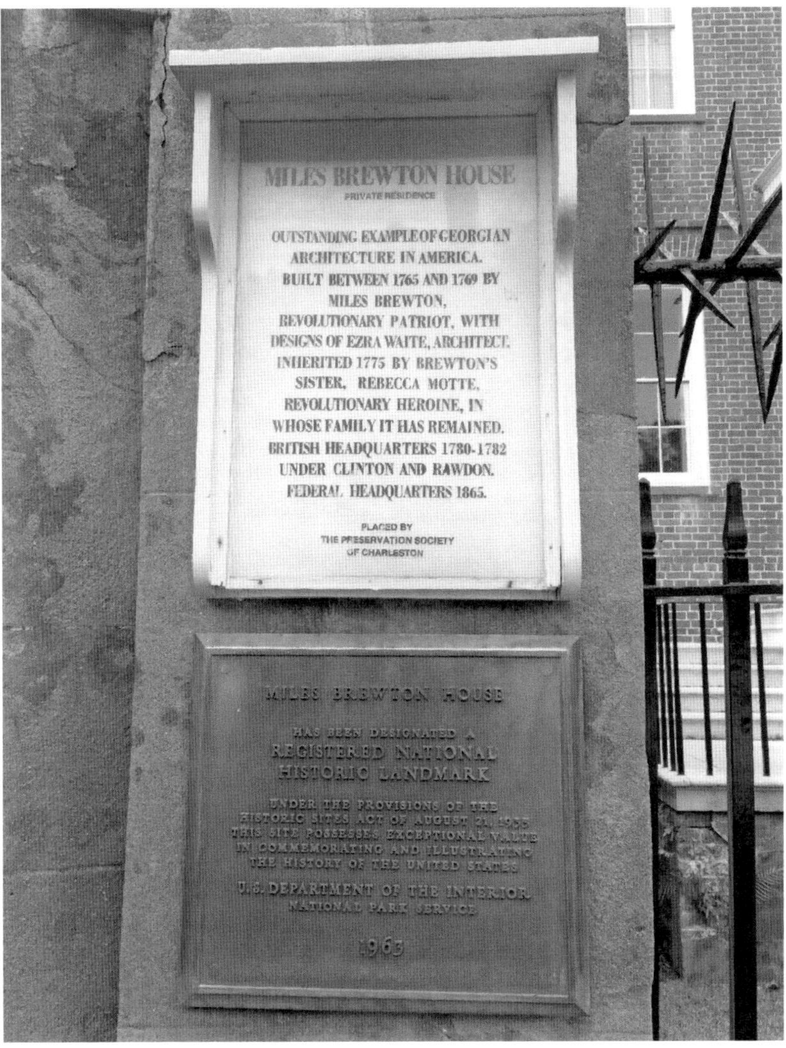

Historic markers at the Miles Brewton House explain its eighteenth-century architectural and historical significance in Charleston. *Photo by author.*

On May 12, around noon, the flaming arrows were shot and the house set afire. The British ran to the roof to put the fire out, but American artillery prevented that response. The English commander immediately surrendered their arms to the Patriots. In an almost fairy tale ending, both the Americans and the British banded together to save the house from being completely engulfed in flame. Mrs. Motte was so thrilled that she gave a dinner for the officers of both sides.

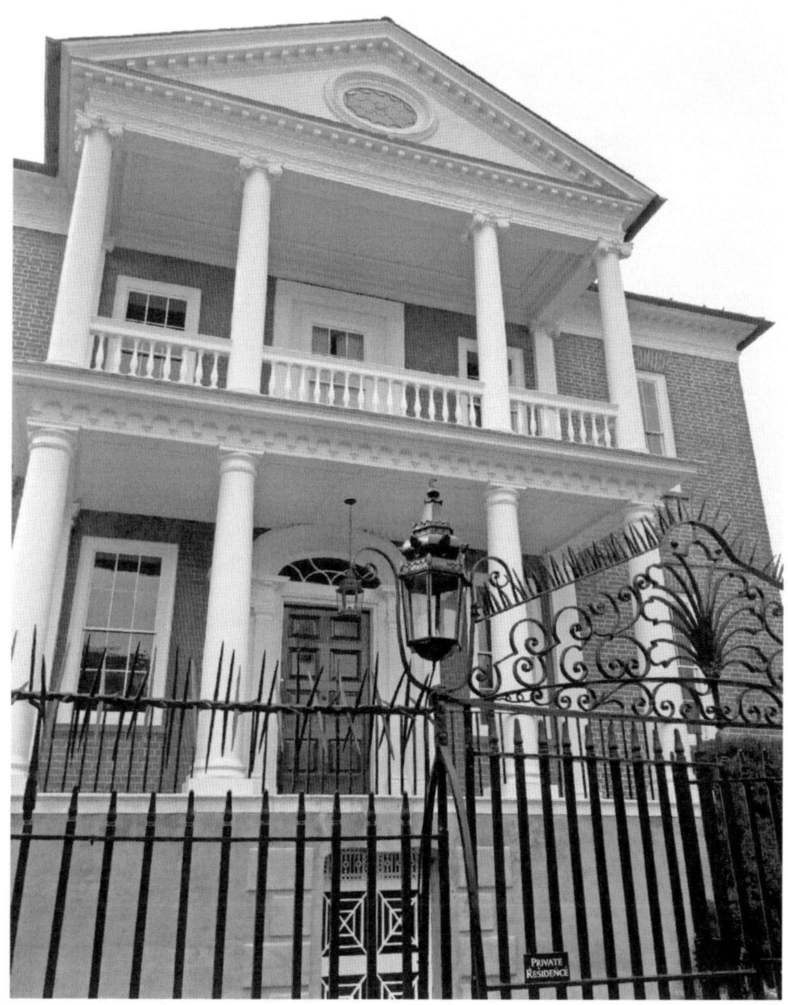

The Miles Brewton House was the family home of Revolutionary heroine Rebecca Brewton Motte. The house also served as Clinton and Rawdon's headquarters in Charleston from 1780 to 1782. *Photo by author.*

At this point, the British held only Georgetown, Augusta, Ninety-Six, Savannah and Charleston. Greene thought that it was time to besiege Ninety-Six and threaten Augusta. Ninety-Six was the westernmost post that Cornwallis had established after taking Charleston in 1780. The location was important for a number of reasons. It was directly halfway from their headquarters in Charleston and the Cherokee Nation—ninety-six miles to be precise.

The South Carolinians in the area were also mostly loyal to the Crown and had made up a force of five hundred for the Loyalist militia. The garrison at Ninety-Six was actually completely made up of Loyalists. The Americans had begun operations much before Greene arrived in May. In fact, after Rawdon evacuated from Camden, he wanted to withdraw from Ninety-Six, too, fearing that it was too exposed in the tumultuous countryside. Rawdon had dispatched messengers to both Ninety-Six and Augusta with instructions to evacuate and retreat to Charleston. All of the messengers were captured by militia and, therefore, did not know they were to leave.[55]

On May 22, 1781, Greene and one thousand men arrived at Ninety-Six, and Pickens and Lee arrived at Augusta. Sumter was to watch the British in Charleston to make sure they did not attempt to reinforce the forts. Greene found Ninety-Six to be a formidable post, with trenches and a stockade surrounding the entire village. There was an additional bunker inside in the shape of an octagonal star.

Greene did not know quite what to do with this seemingly unconquerable fort. He had his men begin to dig approaches, which did not work, and then he had them attack the fort at the star, which was an even worse idea. While the men dug the approaches to the star, Lee and Pickens took Augusta.

The operation in Augusta was quick and not very costly, and they marched back to Ninety-Six on June 6 to assist Greene with his mission. He needed all the help he could get, as hard ground and a limited number of men made the digging process extremely slow. Greene wrote to the President of Congress, "Our poor fellows are worn out being constantly on duty every other day and sometimes every day."[56] While the Americans were digging, the British snipers were firing at the laborers. Greene's men also constructed a tower for his sharpshooters to fire upon the inside of the fort and put a stop to the Tory marksmen.

Rawdon learned of the recent events and left Charleston to help relieve the siege with three new regiments. Greene heard of Rawdon's movements and thought about trying an assault on the fort. He wrote to Sumter, "I believe if we fight a good battle, and if the enemy's force do not exceed 2,500, we shall have a fair prospect of victory."[57] This was a positive thought, but Greene had to make a decision quickly. He doubted that the siege would produce a surrender by the time Rawdon arrived, and Rawdon was moving quickly.

Lee was ordered to the Lowcountry to try to stop Rawdon with the militia of Sumter and Marion. However, they were not moving at all due to complications in Georgetown and the backcountry and could not delay Rawdon as planned. Many of Marion's militiamen heard that they might be going all the way to Ninety-Six, so they deserted. Rawdon was moving at a fast pace from Orangeburg and got out in front of Sumter. Part of his ability to move so quickly was due to a new Tory cavalry unit.

Greene was under a lot of pressure to begin operations on the British post of Ninety-Six quickly, and Lee's arrival back gave him enough men to begin an assault on the water supply of the fort. This attack was successful, and the only way the British inside the fort could get water was to send runaway slaves down to the stream to retrieve it. They were holding on to the hope that Rawdon was on his way.

Greene knew that he had to act quickly, and a surrender seemed unlikely to happen before Rawdon arrived. He could either abandon the siege or attack the post by assault. Greene went ahead with his attack on June 18, 1781, deciding against abandoning the siege. His plan was to attack Ninety-Six on two sides: Lee would attack on one side, and the Continentals would try to get into the star. Lee was successful, but the assault on the other side was met with British bayonets. As the attackers began pulling the sandbags off the fort to make way for the main party of the army, the British arrived. Forty men, two-thirds of the Patriot party, were killed; the operation against the star had failed. Lee's success would have to be halted because they could not hold that small part of the fort. Greene had to call off the attack, and he lifted the siege despite being so close. He wrote on two occasions, "The post is of great importance to the enemy, and our troops have been exposed to excessive labor and annoyance in the attempt. Four more days and the post would have been ours."[58]

Ashamed, Greene sounded the retreat. He held on to hope that surrounding area militia could rally but was still a bit pessimistic like usual. He still wanted to try to force the British out of the backcountry but was worried about the Loyalists in the area.

Greene began to place blame for the failed siege and hoped that he could convince the Continental Congress to send him reinforcements. He was upset with Jefferson for not sending his Virginia militia to assist at Ninety-Six.[59] Greene also targeted the South Carolina militia, questioning the men's patriotism in not fighting for their own state. North Carolina was not safe from Greene's sharp tongue either, as recommendations he was making were overruled by state legislators.

Greene thought it should be his power to appoint state commanders, but administrators were making the calls instead. Interestingly, he did not place blame on who most likely deserved it. Marion was slow to arrive, Sumter could not stop Rawdon and Greene's engineer chose the wrong strategy to attack the fort. Greene was not pleased with Ninety-Six and feared repercussion.

On the positive side, his army had survived, and Greene did actually convince Rawdon that he could not hold Ninety-Six and the surrounding area. Rawdon had no support posts, and he was sure that another Patriot siege would come. He made preparations to return to Charleston, just as Greene had hoped he would. Rawdon took all Loyalists with him south of the Congaree River and promised protection and homes on the plantations that he had seized around Charleston.

On June 27, he convinced them to join him by stating that all loyal to the king were to go or be branded a traitor. This directive did not end well for the Loyalists, who arrived and were told that they would not have any confiscated lands and instead be forced into a wretched town, Rawdonville.

Greene had retreated to Charlotte but used Lee's Legion for intelligence on the happenings of Ninety-Six. After the British gave up on trailing them, Greene returned to Ninety-Six. He hoped to gather local militiamen and destroy everything in the area so that the British could not return. Rawdon had only taken a small force of infantry and cavalry with him as he rushed toward Orangeburg and the hope of reinforcements from another commander, British Colonel Alexander Stewart.

The exiled Loyalists would follow behind with the rest of the men and Tory militia. Greene learned that Stewart would be meeting with Rawdon and ordered William Washington and Lee's cavalry to intercept the supply train. Washington, while keeping an eye on the British, intercepted a message from Stewart to Rawdon stating that Stewart had stopped at Fort Dorchester on the way to meet him. British officials in Charleston told Stewart to stay in the area in case rumored French attacks on the city were to materialize. Rawdon would not get the message that there would be no meeting on July 3, so Greene wanted to take advantage of the situation that was now in front of him.

He immediately ordered the main body of his army to pursue Rawdon, who was heading to Charleston from Ninety-Six, in hopes of attacking the weak and isolated British force, which would be caught off guard and unprepared. Marion and Sumter were to meet with Greene on the other side of the British in the hopes of trapping Rawdon in between the two American forces. Rawdon had no idea the that Americans were planning this ensnarement but was moving quickly and reached the rendezvous point two days earlier than expected. However, the Americans were waiting.

British dragoons had ventured out to forage for food, and the entire group was ambushed and captured. Rawdon knew how dire his situation was without the cavalry, so he hurried toward Stewart as fast as he could. Lee joined in to try to stop the British advance as well by burning a key bridge across the Congaree, but Rawdon was able to get around Lee and arrive in Orangeburg. This march had been very strenuous and taxing on the British; the men were exhausted and dehydrated from the South Carolina summer. Fifty of the soldiers died and those remaining demanded a respite.[60] Greene's men fared not much better and asked for the same.

It was during especially taxing times such as these that Greene wished more than ever that he could be home with his family. His wife shared the same sentiments. Even when Greene was so far away from her, Caty Greene never stopped writing or trying to visit. When he was stationed up north, Caty would visit often and charm all the other officers in the camp. She would throw parties and dinners, and everyone loved having her there. She was not content to stay at home with the children without Nathanael, so she was always itching to join him in the excitement of camp. She even tried to come visit Greene in South Carolina in the summer of 1781. She wrote asking to visit, but Greene felt it was too dangerous. He wrote:

> *The confusion and disorder which has prevailed in Virginia must make you very happy that you did not come to the Southward. There is but few places in North Carolina but that you would require a guard to secure you from the insults and villiany of the Tories. South Carolina and Georgia have been the seat, and are still, of a hot and bloody war. It is true our separation has been long and my wishes are equally strong with yours for a happy meeting; nor shall any thing prevent it a moment longer than the safety of your person requires. It will be my wish that you should come to the southward this fall, if the state of the war will admit, and there is a probability of our meeting. If not, you had better be at home.*[61]

Greene thought of Caty often and was upset he could not be with her. Caty desperately wanted to have a normal family and would often bring her children to camp. The war weighed heavily on Caty as much as it did her husband. Unfortunately, even after the war was over, their life would never be what she wanted.

Greene had to still focus on the task at hand and wished to defeat the British before Rawdon and Stewart met up, so he sent Marion to set a trap for Stewart. The ambush would be on the road from Orangeburg to Monck's Corner, but Stewart never even took that road and passed Marion. Marion sent another cavalry commander, Peter Horry, to chase after Stewart but was only able to capture a few supply wagons.

Stewart and Rawdon finally met up on July 8, 1781. Greene did not lose hope of defeating them and wished to push the British into Charleston for good and eventually out of the entire state. He called on everything he had: one thousand men along with Washington, Marion and Sumter. They reached Orangeburg but decided that they could not attack the post, so they tried to lure Rawdon to them. He did not bite, so Greene retreated to rest his army for a while. For most of July and August, Greene rested his men in the High Hills of the Santee in the middle of the state.

Greene reflected on Ninety-Six and consequent actions and declared that the campaign had been a success despite the loss. He wrote to Thomas McKean, president of the Continental Congress, and reported on the recent events:

> *I did myself the honor to address your excellency on the 22nd of June at Little River near Ninety-Six. Since which we have been constantly upon the move. The enemy pursued us two days, but as our sick, wounded, and Stores had all been sent off before, they could effect nothing, tho' they came on as light as possible, leaving even their Knapsacks and Blankets behind them. We got intelligence by an intercepted Letter that Colo Stewart with a reinforcement was convoying a quantity of Provision and Stores from Charles Town to Lord Rawdon. Unfortunately we were too late they formed their junction without interruption. By late European intelligence I think it highly probably the Enemy will relinquish their operations in Virginia and attempt to recover the entire possession of the two Southern States. I hope the measures I took for the defence of that State will meet the approbation of Congress.*[62]

The British were forced out of the interior of the state and back into the Lowcountry. Greene was also still completely fearful that Cornwallis would try to take South Carolina back. A restful summer would eventually lead to a bloodbath. What was about to come was the last major battle in the South during the American Revolution.

Chapter 4

"A MOST OBSTINATE AND BLOODY ACTION"

Dear Sir, We have a most obstinate and bloody action. Victory was ours.
—Greene to George Washington on the Battle of Eutaw Springs

These were the words written by Nathanael Greene upon the end of the Battle of Eutaw Springs. Greene's words captured the essence of the Battle of Eutaw Springs, one of the costliest battles of the Revolutionary War. Greene's southern campaigns had been particularly dramatic up until this point, as he had an army that had suffered two devastating defeats before he even took charge and transformed the campaign.

It can be noted that Greene overcame more than most generals would have upon receiving command. As previously stated, his army was in a terrible condition, as his men lacked the proper equipment and clothing and had no food and some deserted because of the lack of necessities. Despite the equipment problems, Greene had been able to turn this disheveled band of ruffians into an effective fighting force with new discipline and training strategies. Despite his initial success with his inherited men, he would always struggle to keep his army clothed, fed, equipped and present for duty.

The summer of 1781 proved uneventful for Greene and his men. After the tactically unsuccessful Siege of Ninety-Six, he decided to give his army a six-week respite in the High Hills of the Santee River. Despite losing the siege, Greene was triumphant in one key aspect: Rawdon and the British were forced closer to the coast in the Charleston area, and Greene was one step closer to reaching his goal of ridding South Carolina of the British for good. The operation at Ninety-Six had taken a toll on both armies, and Rawdon himself was in such poor health that he gave up command and left for England. Alexander Stewart took over both armies and rested his weary men around Charleston. However, something brought the British back to the Midlands from the Lowcountry one last time.

Stewart received news that Greene was breaking his rest and marching his men toward Charleston. Greene had hoped to engage the British once more before Cornwallis possibly sent reinforcements and returned to South Carolina.[63] This plan was still a risky move for Greene. If the impending siege at Yorktown was unsuccessful for the Patriots, Cornwallis could move farther south, and it would be up to Greene's army to block his retreat. That would leave him in between Cornwallis and Stewart, who could easily destroy him. Greene needed to strike Stewart quickly and cripple the army enough to prevent another attack. Stewart also decided that he would meet Greene instead of waiting for him and risking the chance to be penned in Charleston by Greene and his men. Both armies consisted of about two thousand men. The heat was extreme in late August, so marching would only happen in the early morning and evening. On August 30, 1781, Greene reached Howell's Ferry on the Congaree River, while Stewart moved to Eutaw.[64] After their long rest, the Patriot forces were ready and eager to eliminate the British. Greene, however, worried and assumed that Stewart's sudden movement meant he was preparing for battle against the Patriots, so Greene put out a call to arms and requested reinforcements. He wrote to Francis Marion on September 5:

> *I beg you will please to form a junction with us as soon as possible; and with our collective force I think we can give a good account of them. It was my intention to attack the enemy at Thomsons, but they retird from there with great precipitation. Since which I am told they are reinforced, otherwise I should not wait your arrival.*[65]

As it turned out, Stewart had no idea that Greene was so close. Resting behind a rising river, the British army had not been gathering intelligence reports and had only moved to that area to protect provisions coming up from Charleston.[66] The Patriots had been actively disrupting these lines of communication and supplies, and rather than splitting up his already weak army to secure the lines, the British commander kept his army together and moved everyone toward Eutaw.

On the evening of September 7, 1781, Greene began preparation for the impending meeting by moving to Burdall's Plantation, seven miles north of

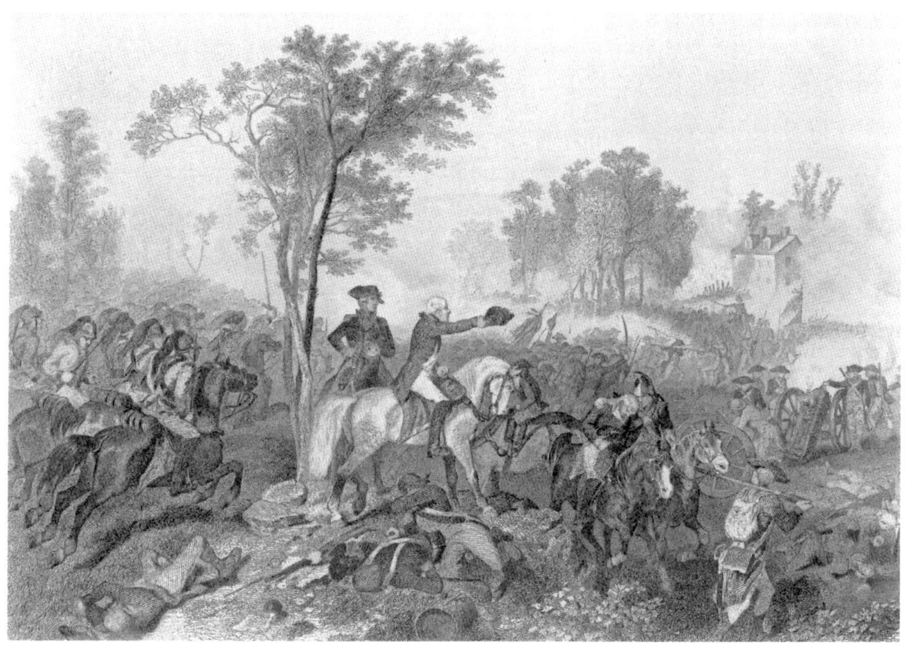

The Battle of Eutaw Springs. Steel engraving that depicts General Greene pointing his army onward on the morning of September 8, 1781. Original painting by Chappel, published by Johnson, Fry and Company in New York, 1859. *Library of Congress.*

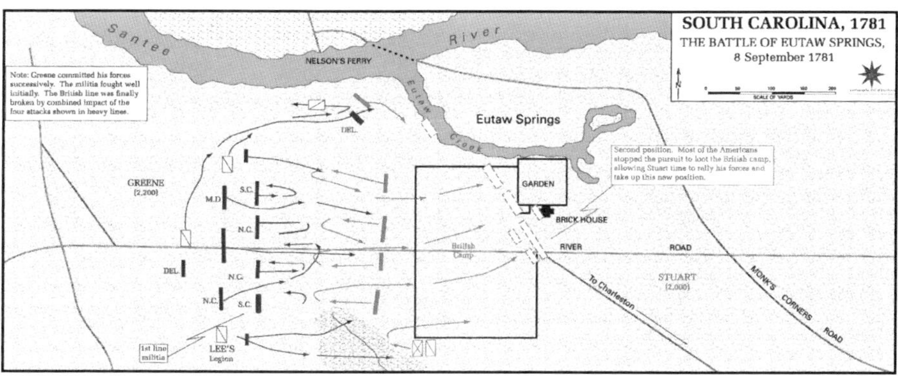

Military movements at the Battle of Eutaw Springs, September 8, 1781. *Courtesy of the United States Military Academy.*

Eutaw. The next morning, at 4:00 a.m., the Patriots continued marching toward the British camp with about 2,300 men lined up in four columns. Lee's Legion led the way, with the South Carolina State Troops immediately following under the command of William Henderson. Next was Francis Marion's Carolina militia; third was Continentals from Maryland, North Carolina and Virginia; and bringing up the rear were William Washington's dragoons, only to be used if absolutely necessary.[67]

Greene's strategy was to be overly cautious by marching slowly so that the group could stay together and surprise the British. This proved to be productive. Stewart heard that Greene's army was nearby when two American deserters reported its position. He sent out some dragoons to investigate, only to find that the report was true by way of an ambush, which cost Stewart one hundred men. Also, early that morning, he had sent out unarmed men to forage for sweet potatoes, and they, in turn, were also captured. Alarmed, Stewart leapt into action and sent men out to meet Greene and halt his advance to prepare for battle. He bought himself some time to prepare for battle, but Stewart wasn't worried now.

His army was composed of veterans who had seen one or two surprises before. They quickly moved into battle formation across the path of the advancing Patriot army. Greene's line looked very similar to his Cowpens arrangement, with the first line comprising the militia and with Marion and Pickens on either side. The second line was composed of Continentals, with Lieutenant Colonel Wade Hampton, commander of a South Carolina volunteer cavalry regiment, and Lee's horsemen and artillery protecting them.[68]

Greene was never a big fan of the militia, finding the men unreliable and uncontrollable, but he would have no complaints about them at Eutaw Springs. He wrote to George Washington, "The militia fought with a degree of Spirit and firmness that reflects the highest honor upon this class of soldier."[69]

The Americans advanced into firing range, and Marion's band was able to fire off seventeen rounds before the men were forced back by the British, who largely outnumbered them. Greene ordered his Continentals to steady the line, and Stewart sent in his infantry reserves. The Continentals wavered under the attack of the superior British guns, and the line began to fall once again. The British took this setback to mean a victory and broke their line to pursue the Americans. Greene reacted quickly, showing his adeptness in reading battlefields, and ordered the rest of the Continentals to advance, firing at a distance of forty yards, and jump into a bayonet charge.[70] This caused the British left side to collapse, and the Americans captured three hundred of their men and two of their cannons. It looked like Stewart was beaten and Greene would be a hero. Now they just needed to prevent the British from rallying.

Greene was not about to let that happen and ordered one of his commanders, William Washington, to attack the grenadiers with his cavalry.

However, the brush was too dense for the horses to get through, and they were met with murderous fire from the British ranks. Washington was wounded, pinned under his dead horse and taken prisoner. He was sent to Charleston, held under house arrest and remained there until the end of the war. Only two of the officers of the cavalry made it back unharmed. The British found their way to a brick mansion behind their camp, where they and their Loyalist comrades were able to send heavy fire into the advancing Patriots.[71] It became a race to the mansion; the Patriots were so close behind the British that the door had to be closed on some of their own officers and men. More of the British found their way to the garden behind the house and were able to rally. Greene wrote to George Washington about this particular movement, "Nothing but the brick house, and the peculiar strength of the position at Eutaw saved the remains of the British Army from being all made prisoners."[72]

However, the British also had time to rally because Greene's troops started to ignore couth and decorum and lost all order to raid the British encampment. They found plunder, food, provisions, liquor and clothing. The soldiers—who were thirsty, tired, hungry and partially naked—could

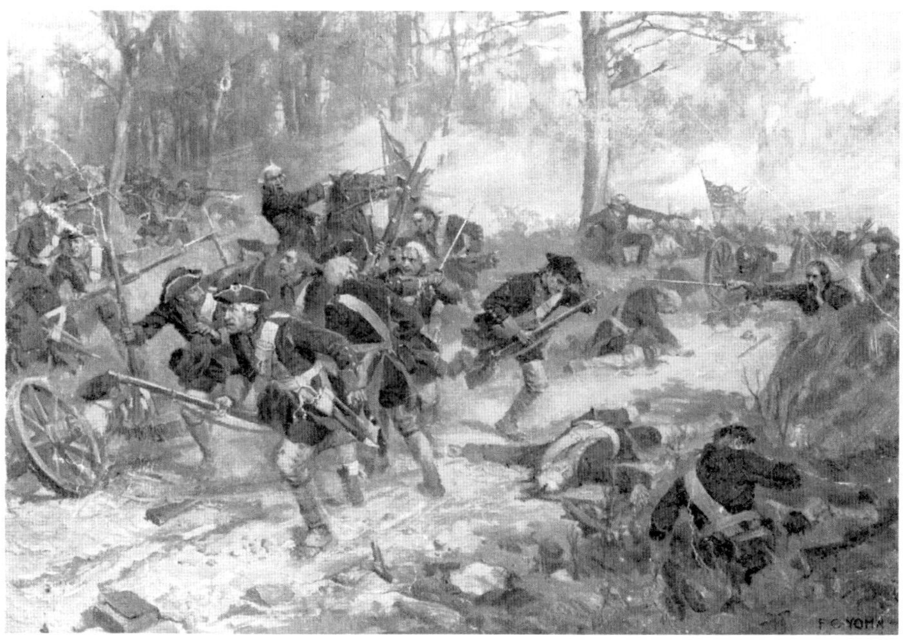

The Battle of Eutaw Springs by Frederick Coffay Yohn. Image depicts the American army breaking the British line. *Courtesy of the New York Public Library.*

not help themselves. The officers continued to lead a charge through the camp to the house but quickly noticed that their men were forming a mob as they looted Stewart's camp. The soldiers forgot themselves as they drank in the liquors and refreshments, and all order was lost. A sure victory was slipping through Greene's grasp.

There were two British units left on the field, and Lee and his cavalry were sent to attack. The British cavalry responded by attacking the Patriot infantry, who were still looting the tents. Luckily, the South Carolina horsemen were able to stop the British cavalry and send them away.[73] Another British unit disrupted a second American cavalry unit, while American cannons boomed toward the brick house. Unable to breach the walls, they moved closer only to be gunned down by the Loyalist marksmen. Greene's infantrymen were not able to reform, and after hours of fighting in the intense heat, both armies had had enough.

They collected their wounded from around the area but had to leave the men who were closest to the brick mansion. Greene retreated the seven miles back to Burdall's Plantation because they could not find fresh water any place closer than that and his troops desperately needed it.[74] He reported that his decision to retreat was forced on him because they ran out of ammunition and that another attack would have been fruitless. Stewart, for his part, wrote that his reason for stopping the battle was the lack of remaining cavalry. Additionally, he did not need to pursue the Americans because he could claim victory as the enemy ran from the field in disarray.

Greene viewed that the Battle of Eutaw Springs as a win for the Patriots. Greene wrote to George Washington of the battle:

> *Since I wrote you before we have had a most bloody Battle. It was by far the most Obstinate fight I ever saw. Victory was ours, and had it not been for one of those little incidents which frequently happen in the progress of War, we should have taken the whole brittish Army. Nothing could exceed the gallantry of our officers or the bravery of our troops.*[75]

Greene was not only claiming victory over the British but also that he could have taken the entire army. It is difficult to say which side was the victor of Eutaw Springs, as both sides claimed it and suffered heavy casualties. Greene's casualty count on American forces was 574, including 119 killed, 383 wounded and 78 missing. Of his officers, 17 were killed and 43 wounded. Greene repeatedly claimed that he took 500 prisoners on that day, but Stewart's numbers were different. Stewart claimed 85 men dead, 351 wounded and 257 missing.

"There has been some question concerning Stewart's figures," Conrad wrote, "especially since he used the 'victory' at Eutaw to argue that he deserved a promotion to Brigadier General."[76] While the numbers prove difficult to determine a victor, the strategic results are far easier to discern.

Greene wrote to Harry Lee in October that his objectives for the Battle of Eutaw Springs were to maintain an aura of superiority, to remove Stewart from the Congaree, to stop him from threatening Patriot lines of communications and supplies, to force the British back to Charleston, to intercept Cornwallis should he come and to ultimately force them out of South Carolina.[77] In these goals, Greene was most successful.

He wrote a number of letters to fellow leaders that he wished he had been able to destroy the British army completely, but staying true to his character, he did not want to risk losing more of his men to accomplish this goal. Even his engaging the British at Eutaw Springs was not at all risky, as Greene knew that his strength in cavalry was superior to the British so ultimately he would not have a disaster on his hands. He knew he only had a few months until many of his regular troops' contracts would end, so he needed to strike a blow at Stewart soon that would devastate his numbers more than his own. The events that took place immediately after Eutaw Springs proved once again that Nathanael Greene was a strategic mastermind.

On September 9, 1781, Stewart retreated from Eutaw in great haste and with little care. The British destroyed much of their supplies, including all of the liquor and one thousand arms, which were thrown in the creek. The Patriots managed to salvage three hundred of these arms. Additionally, Stewart left behind about seventy of his injured men. Another British officer, Major Archibald McArthur, joined Stewart as reinforcement but was advised to not return to the field. The British fled all the way to Moncks Corner and their post at Dorchester, virtually ending British control of South Carolina except for Charleston and the Lowcountry. Greene wrote of the action to the Marquis de Lafayette:

> *We obtained a complete victory and had it not been for one of those incidents to which military operations are subject we should have taken the whole british Army; however we took 500 prisoners and killed and wounded a much greater number, and have driven the Enemy almost to the gates of Charles Town.*[78]

While Stewart was retreating to Charleston, where the British would stay for the remainder of the war, Greene went on the offensive to try to pursue

Stewart into Charleston and stop McArthur from joining Stewart. This was unsuccessful, but Greene knew that Stewart would have to stay near Charleston, so he took his men to rest in the High Hills of the Santee.

The British would stay on the defensive for the next year, as Greene had the upper hand. Charlestonian David Ramsay, one of the first historians of the American Revolution, discovered that "after Eutaw, the British no more acted with their usual vigor. On the slightest appearance of danger, they discovered a disposition to flee scarcely inferior to what was exhibited the year before by the American militia."[79] For the Patriots, victory seemed to be assured, but for Greene, self-preservation and keeping pressure on the British forces outside Charleston became his most pressing issues.

At camp, Greene went back to his usual problems of lacking supplies. His first concern was medical supplies for his wounded troops. This shortage was a problem for all of the American commanders, as they lacked medicines and supplies for hospitals all over. The situation became critical as fever and other epidemics spread through the armies. Greene had made a habit of visiting hospitals to cheer up the wounded men. When he visited after Eutaw Springs sometime in late September/early October, he was disgusted with what he saw. Men were everywhere, suffering from wounds sustained in battle but also from the horrible conditions they had to recover in with no supplies. He wrote to Congress, "It is deplorable that numbers of brave fellows who have bled in the cause of their country have been eaten up with maggots, and perished in that miserable state."[80]

This situation improved slightly with medical supplies finally being delivered and milder weather approaching, but Greene and the hospitals would struggle with getting supplies through the end of the war. This lack of supplies was just one of the challenges Greene would have as he fought to remove the British from Charleston. It was part of a larger problem in which Greene lacked everything he needed. He did not have enough food or clothing for his army, and he always feared mutiny among the troops because of that lack of necessities. The root of his troubles was because he lacked money in general. By the end of 1781, the paper money that the state and national governments had printed was worthless. South Carolina, North Carolina and Georgia all struggled with financial problems, while colonies north of Maryland had a more stable currency and economic prosperity.

The South did not have the money to buy needed items, but no supplies were available, as manufactured goods were in short supply. Greene and others were forced to barter for things they needed using indigo and salt. This practice did not go unnoticed, as the superintendent of finance, Robert

Morris, wrote to Greene applauding him for his ingenuity in finding ways to provide for his troops.[81] Morris tried to help by using monies from the National Bank, but southerners would not put their money in this bank.

This occurrence, among others, is what caused Greene to get heavily involved in politics in 1782. He believed that a strong national government with the ability to raise money was absolutely necessary. Greene tried everything he could to make something out of nothing for his troops and wrote many harsh letters to military officials to support the army better. Not everyone received these letters well, and Greene found himself in the middle of controversy for the last days of his command of the South. The shortages would continue throughout the whole next year despite Greene's efforts.

After the Battle of Eutaw Springs, Greene was able to almost retire completely from large-scale battles. While the battles were over, Greene's men engaged in a number of skirmishes with the British on the outskirts of Charleston. The British were still strong and completely capable of beating the weakened Patriot forces. Greene became heavily involved in the politics of South Carolina to advocate for the support of the army and suggest legislative action to make South Carolina function peacefully. But before Greene could turn his complete attention to building a strong national government, he first had to eliminate the British army and recapture Charleston, which was a process that would take up until December 1782 to complete.

Chapter 5

"WE SHALL HAVE THE DEVIL TO PAY"

Col Laurens wrote me last night that by good intelligence from Charles Town he had great reason to believe a large reinforcement was on their passage from New York and within a day or two sail of Charles Town. Should the report be true we shall have the devil to pay.

—Greene to Lee in December 1781

The last year of Greene's command of the Southern Army was critical in keeping the British contained to Charleston. If he failed to keep his army in fighting condition, all of his gains could have been lost. Historians have glossed over this year, making assumptions as to why Greene emerged victorious without delving into his correspondences and orders of 1782. He still had a strong British force to contain and a weakened army to maintain and supply. With South Carolina in a state of financial exhaustion and goods not being available for purchase, Greene tried to get more supplies for his men.

In the fall and winter of 1781–82, he was completely on his own and forced to use his own money to satisfy the needs of his army. Not only did he lack supplies for his men, but he also lacked adequate numbers of soldiers to pressure the British in Charleston. Because of his frustrations, he became an outspoken advocate for strengthening the national government, but his voice was not universally welcome. As a result, his final days as commander were filled with political controversy.

One of Greene's great allies was Thomas Burke, governor of North Carolina. They corresponded on many occasions, agreeing about the need for a strong national government.[82] They also shared the belief of supporting the Continental army as much as possible. However, Greene lost his friend when the British captured him and removed him from office.

Burke had been working up a plan to attack Wilmington and remove the hub of Loyalist activity from the Carolinas. However, the Loyalists struck first and captured Burke and two hundred other Patriots in September 1781. This victory lifted the spirits of Loyalists in North and South Carolina, and Greene called one of his generals to put down Loyalist rebellions. This mission was successful, as the Loyalists were dispersed in the Pee Dee region of South Carolina.

However, issues with the Loyalists took a turn in the aftermath of the defeat and involved Greene in controversy. One of the militia generals, Griffith Rutherford, wished to completely put an end to Loyalist resistance, so he drove through Tory territory. Greene learned that Rutherford was employing a scorched-earth policy, which angered him. He wrote immediately to Rutherford condemning these tactics, stating, "I would always recommend moderation, not from any regard to the Tories, but for our own sakes, cruelty being dishonorable and persecution always increasing the number and force of our enemies."[83]

Greene was a true nationalist and proposed a policy toward the Loyalists that would help the country move forward. Rutherford wrote back later saying that his actions were lawful and necessary.[84] This issue of how to treat the Tories would not go away for Greene. He stayed true to his nationalist beliefs and always encouraged moderation when the legislators often called for vengeance.

Greene's attitudes and policies toward Loyalists were part of a larger and longer problem in the southern colonies. Some South Carolinians, such as Thomas Sumter, believed that there was no way to have peace after the conflict ended, so punishing the Loyalists and forcing them to leave seemed like the only way to handle the issue. Additionally, those sharing this viewpoint found that they could seize land, property and money from Loyalists to solve their own financial woes.

This area is one in which Greene became involved in politics in the southern states. However, Greene's opinions were often met with opposition. Although the war between George Washington and Cornwallis had ended in the trenches outside Yorktown in October 1781, the war was not yet won. People became uneasy about the war and were not sure where the colonies stood just after the surrender. Some Loyalists could not believe the news and felt that British rule in the colonies could still be saved.[85] Greene called the removal of some of the British a mixed blessing. He believed that the remaining British strength was concentrated, while Patriot strength had been dispersed:[86] "After Britain ceased nearly all offensive operations in January 1782, this was more than ever a civil war, waged by Loyalists and Patriots."[87] South Carolina increasingly had to carry on the struggle of the entire South without help from other states, facing both the remaining British forces and Loyalists.

Before Cornwallis was trapped at Yorktown, Greene planned an operation to remove the British completely from the South. His plan included the French fleet attacking Charleston from the sea and the Patriots coming from land, creating a perfect trap for the British. Greene knew that Charleston was the key to British removal, and the city was an easy target for the French. He wrote to Washington for approval, offering to serve as the subordinate on the mission.[88]

Much to his disappointment, Washington had already asked the French about this plan, and they wrote that they could not remain on the American coast for as long as this plan would take to finish. Greene tried to intercede one last time, arguing that the "suffering of the South claimed every attention."[89] Eventually, the French did approve an attack on Wilmington, but the post had already been evacuated before the French took action. The French would be of no help to Greene in South Carolina. They did eventually send two thousand troops to aid, but they were stationed in Virginia. Conrad remarked, "This blessing emerged as a double-edged sword, because the troops which were to allow Virginia to send additional troops to Greene instead added to a sense of security in Virginia and reduced any feeling of urgency concerning Greene's need for men and material in South Carolina."[90] Greene was again in the position of needing troops and supplies. This problem was not going away soon.

Finally, some good news reached Greene's camp on November 9, 1781. Official news of Cornwallis's October 19 surrender at Yorktown arrived, and there was much rejoicing. Even Francis Marion, who was usually against drinking and excessive merriment, gave a ball. Characteristically, Greene was not celebrating, as he was worried about mounting problems he still faced despite the surrender. His need for men had now reached the critical point, as the militia left for home after Eutaw Springs. His number of regulars was drastically reduced, and their time of service was reaching an end.

Marion, Pickens and Hampton, Greene's most reliable commanders, were no longer with him, as they had been dispatched to help in other parts of the state. Many of Greene's Continentals were ill or wounded, and the healthy ones had to nurse the wounded from Eutaw Springs. He often had

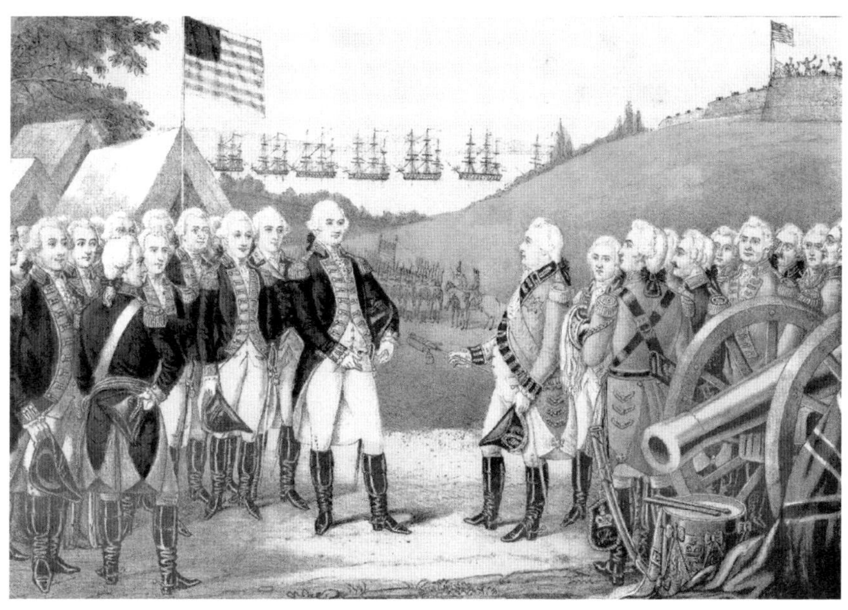

Cornwallis surrenders to Washington on October 19, 1781, at Yorktown. Date and original publication unknown. *Courtesy of Library of Congress.*

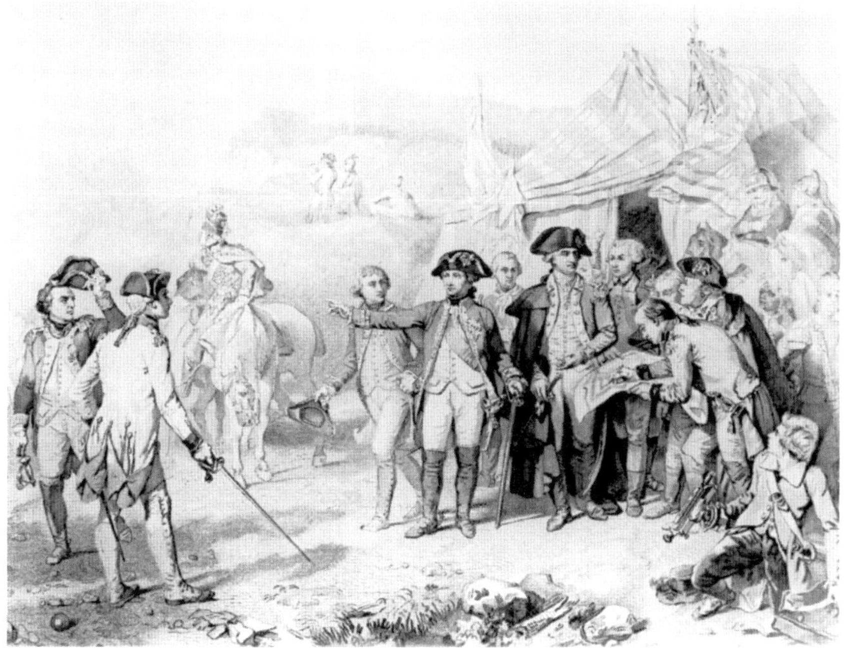

Siege of Yorktown. Engraving by O.M. Fontaine, from painting by Conder. *Courtesy of the National Archives.*

fewer than 1,000 men fit for service, to keep approximately 3,000 British in Charleston in check.[91] Eventually, he did receive some reinforcements from the North after the Yorktown operation. About 1,200 men arrived and joined the army at the end of October.

Nathanael Greene decided to renew the offensive and attempt to drive the British farther into the city of Charleston. At this time, the British front lines were located considerably northwest of Charleston, anchored at Fort Dorchester. Instead of attacking them directly, Greene began to maneuver his troops southeast and use guerrilla warfare to harass the British supply lines.[92] This operation was more successful than Greene could have even imagined.

The plan began with Greene's cavalry misleading the British into stationing themselves at their post at Dorchester. Greene wanted to draw the British from their various locations in the Lowcountry by making them believe that a major attack at Fort Dorchester was coming. Once all of the remaining troops were together in one position, other areas would be free from British control and it would be easier for Greene to push them out of South Carolina for good.

Once they were at Dorchester, the Americans planned to entrench themselves at Four Holes near the British post.[93] Until this point, Marion reported that the

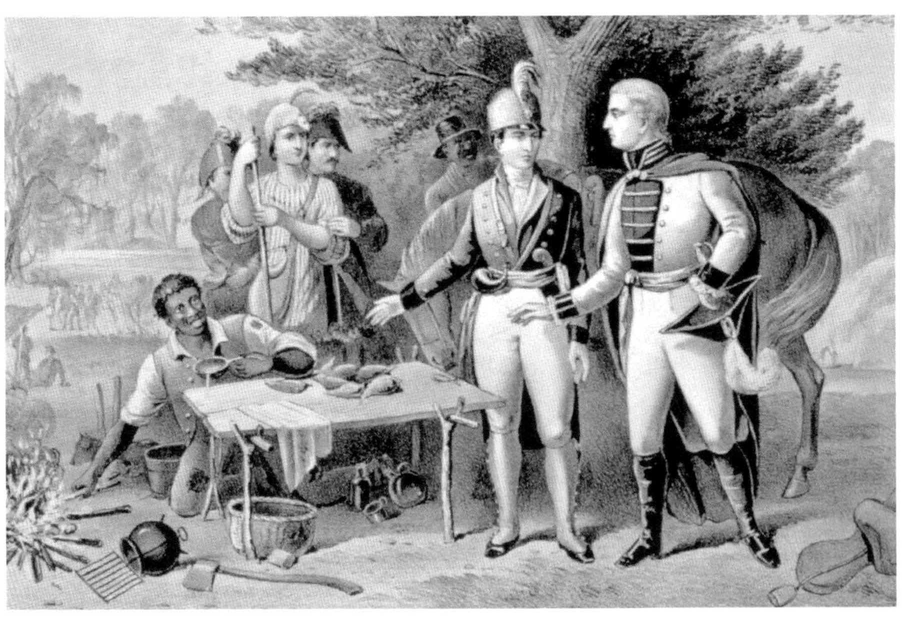

Print showing General Francis Marion offering to share his meal of sweet potatoes and water with a British officer. Published by Currier & Ives, New York, circa 1876. *Courtesy of Library of Congress.*

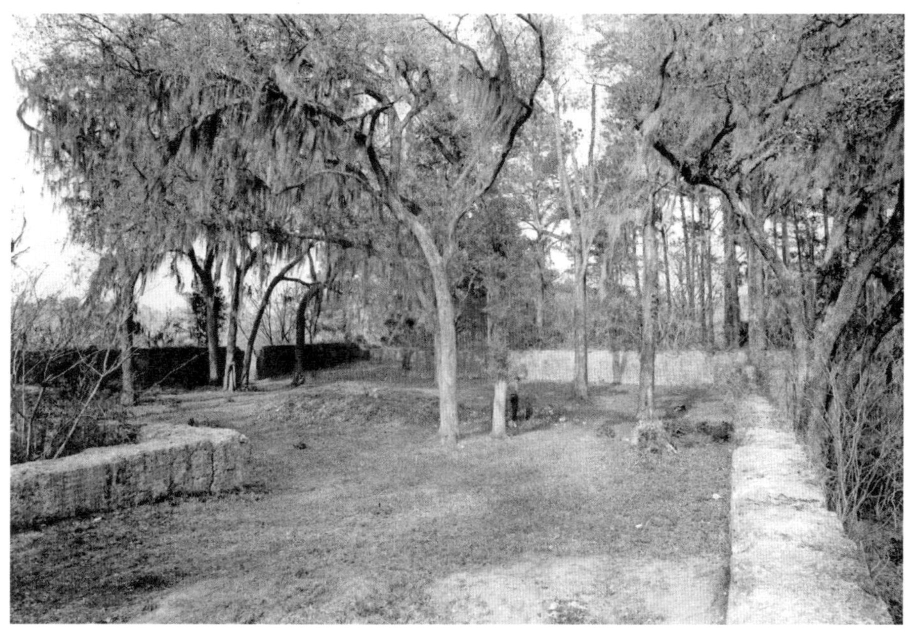

Fort Dorchester ruins in Summerville, South Carolina. Historic American Buildings Survey. *Courtesy of Library of Congress.*

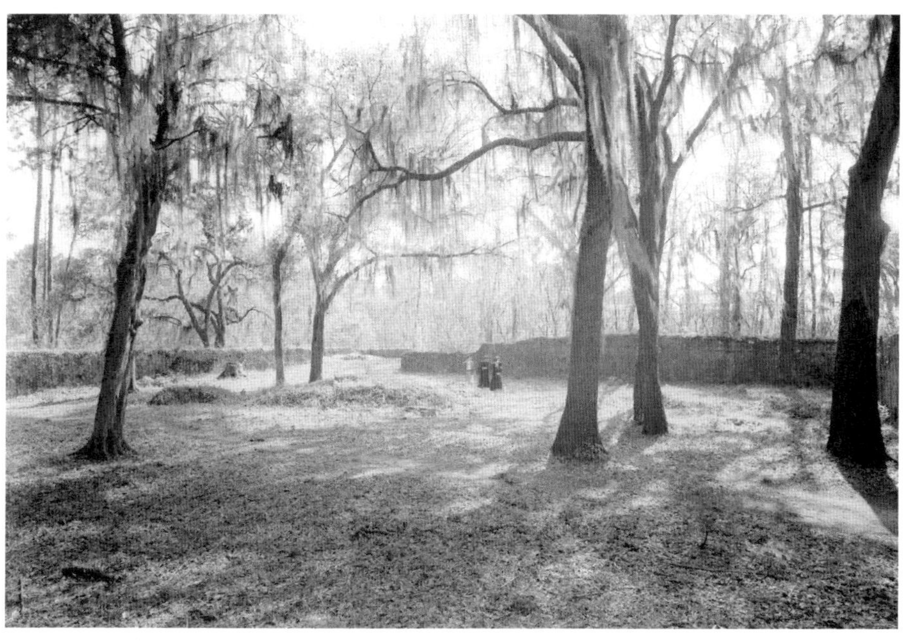

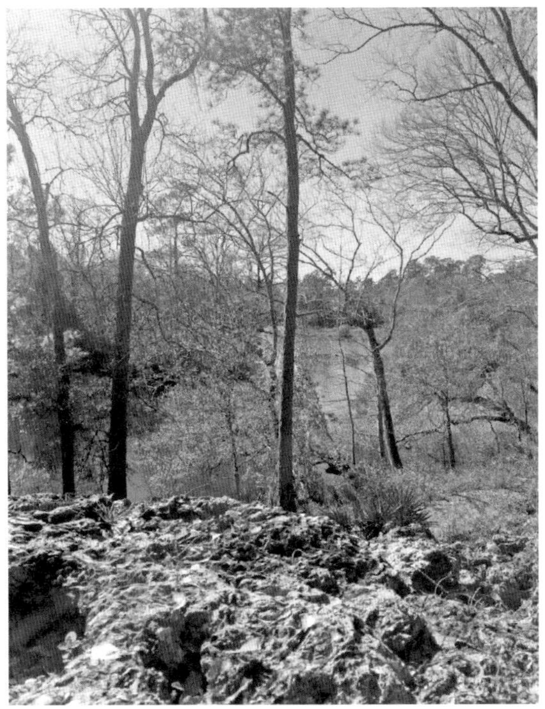

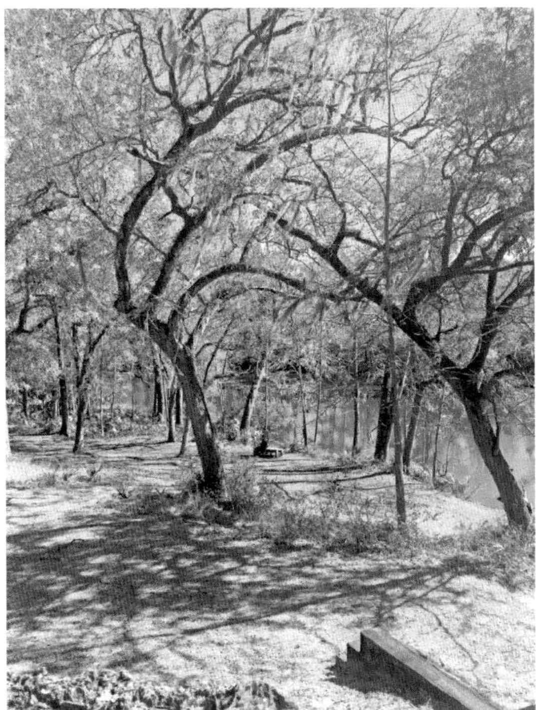

British were plundering and foraging in the area and taking slaves from the Santee River plantations. Sometimes Marion would share his stores with the British officers to keep them from stealing. Marion had thought that they would be heading to Georgia but had no idea what they were planning on doing with the slaves. He guessed that they were planning on arming the slave men to fight the Americans, but they were taking large numbers of women and children, who would not have been of help.[94]

What Marion did not realize was that the British were using women just as much as men. Their duties with the British included making musket cartridges and serving as nurses in hospitals.[95] Once the American cavalry starting moving into the area, the British panicked. They retreated at the first sign of

Left: Views of the Ashley River from Fort Dorchester at Colonial Dorchester State Historic Site in Summerville, South Carolina. *Photo by author.*

American activity, just like Greene hoped, to Fort Dorchester. Marion wrote to Greene, "The enemy left Fair Lawn yesterday morning in great haste and its [*sic*] gone towards town. Two thirds of the [British] mounting men has left. I will follow with Maham this moment near Huger's Bridge if you wish to send any particular commands."[96] Marion tailed the British and hovered around Fort Dorchester until Greene joined him in the area.

The British had problems of their own following Eutaw Springs. They also lacked men and provisions, as the battle had claimed almost one thousand of their number. Additionally, their leadership was lacking, and their morale was very low. Greene had everything in his favor for the upcoming encounter, and that is exactly how he liked it. Greene rarely made risky moves in his operations; his cavalry was stronger, and Marion was keeping an eye on the enemy. Marion again reported to Greene, "The enemy two days ago was below Goose Creek Bridge collecting stock and forage. I have sent 100 cavalry to the enemys line. Ten battus of men came up within four miles of us but returned immediately as they seen my patrolling party. If you should move down I can easyly join you."[97]

On December 1, Greene led the cavalry to survey the situation at Dorchester. Greene knew that the remaining Loyalists were in Charleston and that the British were completely out of the upcountry. His task now was to remove the British from Dorchester and force them into the neck of Charleston. This would be difficult because the fort was located on the Ashley River, leaving an easy escape route for the British. He engaged the enemy in two skirmishes involving the cavalry, and Greene noted that the British were very respectful.[98] The Americans killed a handful of the infantry and cavalry, and Greene was recognized immediately. The post commander, so fearful of Greene and believing that the entire Patriot army was nearby, was completely bewildered. Greene reported the incident to Colonel Williams:

> *I wrote you yesterday of our little skirmish before Dorchester. The enemy evacuated it the same night and burnt their works, stores, and forage and retired to the Quarter House. They appear to have been much alarmed and have disgraced themselves not a little by their precipitate retreat.*[99]

After burning everything, the British abandoned Dorchester for their post on the neck of the Charleston peninsula. Greene had garnered quite a reputation among the British, and this is one example of their changing attitudes at the end of the war. They were completely on the defensive and

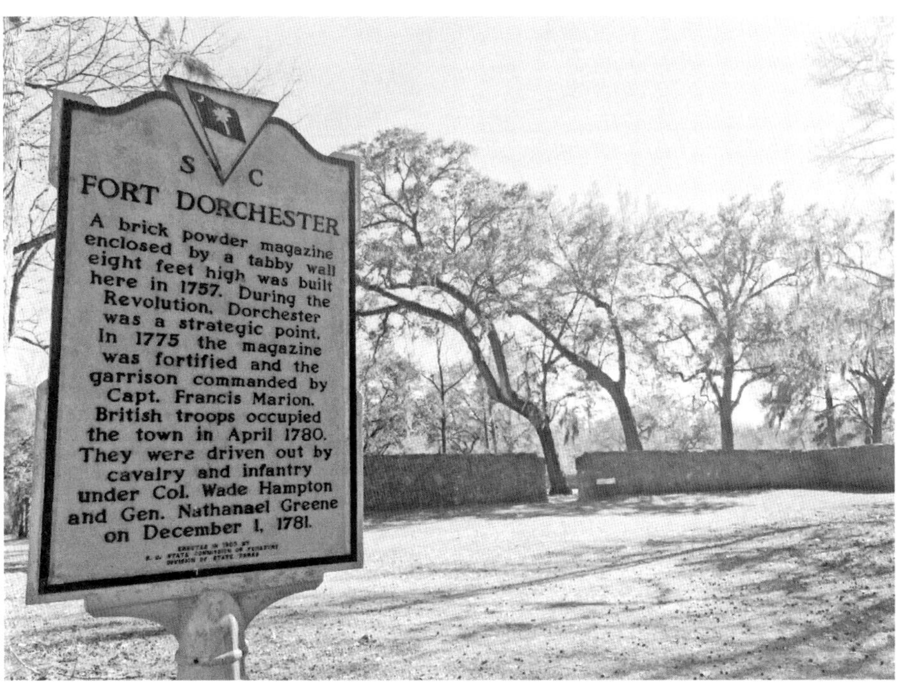

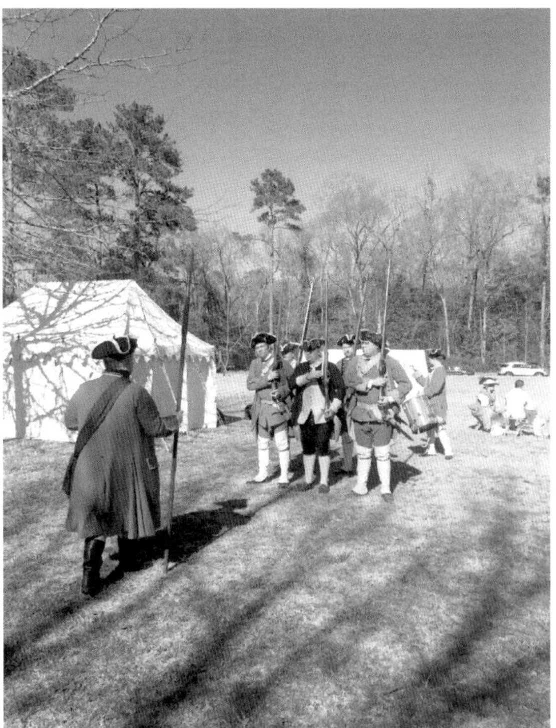

Above: Historic marker outside Fort Dorchester explaining military action of Greene on December 1, 1781, at the site. British fled from their post when they learned that Greene was near. *Photo by author.*

Left: Reenactment of military actions at Colonial Dorchester State Historic Site in Summerville, South Carolina, in February 2016. *Photo by author.*

seemed defeatist in most instances. Greene was satisfied that finally the enemy was mostly penned.

The British had gotten to the point of desperation and began to arm black slaves to defend their post and the Charleston peninsula from the Patriots. Southerners started to view the British as no longer a threat, believing that their arming of slaves showed their weakness. This viewpoint was shared by many Americans and created a major problem for Greene. Although the British had surrendered and evacuated most areas in the colonies, they were still in Charleston and defending the city. Not only were they in Charleston, but they were also stationed in Savannah and the coastal areas in between the cities. Without the support of the public or the government, Greene would not receive the reinforcements or supplies he desperately needed. He hoped that if the general feeling was to support the military, this thinking would eventually trickle up to the Continental Congress and encourage it to send aid. With most Charleston diplomats under house arrest or held elsewhere as prisoners of war, Greene hoped that some of his military peers and small farmers in the backcountry and miles outside Charleston would support his position.

In the last days of 1781, Greene established a Patriot line around the perimeter of Charleston. He sent Marion to the eastern side of the Cooper River to keep the British from Georgetown and continue to disrupt supply and communication lines. Sumter went to Orangeburg and Four Holes to protect the rear of the Patriot force and the supply lines. Hardin was placed south of Charleston, making a complete circle. The key part of Greene's plan was his use of Wade Hampton and his cavalry. By having the horsemen patrol in between the infantry stationed around Charleston, Greene's lines of communication would be preserved, and the cavalry would act as a screen in front of the main body of the army. Conrad noted, "As was common in Greene's operations, Patriot superiority in cavalry was the key to the close investment of the British. The cavalry kept the enemy off balance and gave the Patriots greater mobility, enabling them to collect rapidly to meet British sallies."[100] What was even more important was tricking the British into thinking that the Patriot army was strong when, in reality, it was weaker than it had ever been. At times, three thousand British troops in Charleston were besieged by only eight hundred Patriot men.[101] The truth of the matter for Greene in 1782 is that he was not really able to keep his army together and appropriately supplied, as the government was not sending him reinforcements or provisions. It was Greene's clever use of his mobile cavalry that gave him the edge he needed to deceive the British in Charleston a bit longer.

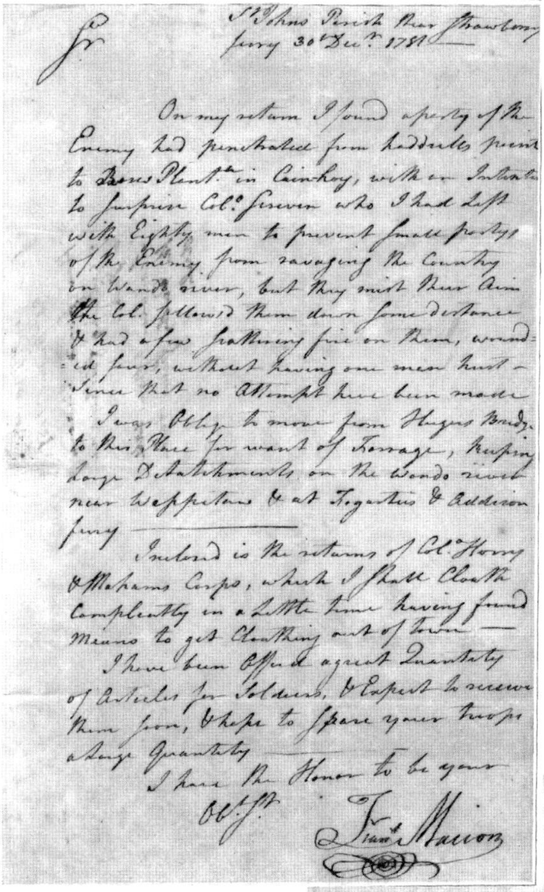

Left: Front page of correspondence from Francis Marion to Greene, dated December 30, 1781. Marion reports on his movements around the perimeter of Charleston. *American Revolutionary War Papers of the Charleston Museum Archives.*

Below: Envelope of correspondence from Francis Marion to Greene, dated December 30, 1781. *American Revolutionary War Papers of the Charleston Museum Archives.*

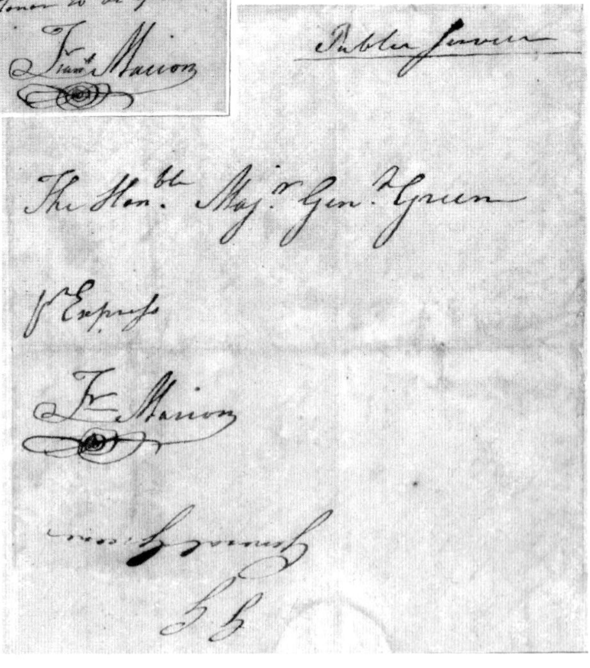

The British retreat in the face of a weak Patriot army encouraged Greene, but he still had major challenges to deal with on his side. As previously stated, the attitude of South Carolinians and other southerners was that of complacency. They felt that they had won the war, as the British were weak and resorting to using slaves as protectors. They also used slaves as laborers, spies and information bases, as they knew certain roads and wooded areas.[102] Meanwhile, Sumter and others were seizing slaves from plantations to distribute as bounties to his troops.[103] Both sides treated the slaves as property to use, sell and claim, but Americans were mostly angry that their slaves would fight against them. Despite what the public thought about the condition of the British army, Greene knew that the war was far from over and that the British were still very dangerous and capable of defeating the weakened Patriot army. Charleston was important to the British for a number of reasons. It was a major port city, and the British used Charleston to import supplies and troops from England and other parts of the colonies. It was their strongest holding in the South, and without it, their position in the South would be desperate.

Additionally, there was the possibility of the British holding on to Charleston even after the war had ended. Gregory Massey, author of a book on John Laurens, explained, "Now an alarming scenario loomed; Greene warned Rutledge that the British ministry might negotiate peace with the Americans on the basis of *uti possidetis*, allowing them to retain all territory held by their army. Under this arrangement, Charleston would remain a British possession."[104] For a year, Greene had to preach to the people that the war was not over yet, that they still needed to force the British out to prevent this from happening. Public support is something Greene desperately needed in order to achieve his mission. In an article on Greene and the importance of public support, James Haw asserted, "Greene's realization of the importance of public support and his actions to maintain it significantly influenced his conduct of the southern campaigns of 1780 to 1782."[105] To make sure his important message was heard at the end of the war, Greene became heavily involved in the politics of South Carolina.

Greene's last days of the war were a tedious job of keeping the British held in Charleston. In July 1782, he wrote, "[O]ur operations this year are as insipid as they were important in the last."[106] The main duty of the Patriots was to limit the British to movements within Charleston without allowing them to spread into the country. This mission is precisely the reason why these small skirmishes mattered. Although this task may seem like it was merely guarding noncombatants, Greene's operations involved constant movement.

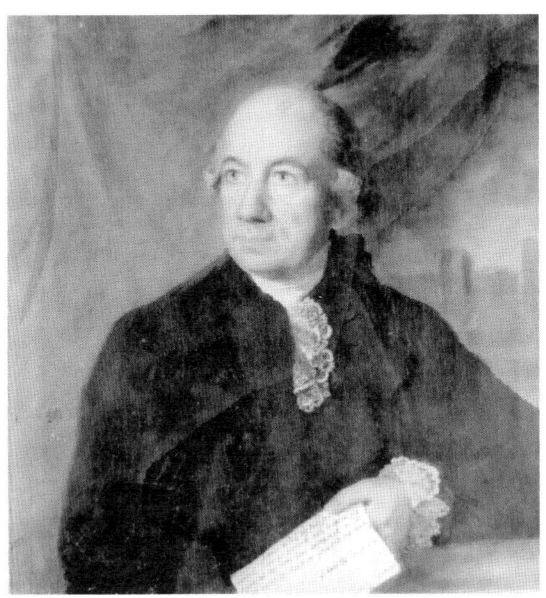

Henry Laurens, painting (bust) by John S. Copley, 1781. *Courtesy of the National Archives.*

While there was not massive bloodshed, there were still some conflicts between the British and Americans resulting in deaths. These skirmishes were mainly with British foraging expeditions, but one did claim the life of notable officer John Laurens, son of wealthy South Carolina politician Henry Laurens, in August 1782. Greene's task was a difficult one because of Charleston's large network of waterways that could allow the British to move about easily and strike with little warning.

Greene was not concerned with starving the British but rather with preventing any offensive movements to recapture additional land outside Charleston. Patriot forces would be no match for the much stronger British army, which could send out detachments. Because of this, Greene instructed his units to move constantly to prevent surprise attacks, protect supplies, stop threats of Tory involvement and make it look like they had enough manpower when they were severely lacking. He often called on Marion to keep the British at bay to prevent them from pushing out of Charleston and to intercept any communication coming to the British from their other stations like Savannah.

Greene was overly cautious in all matters of his life, especially as a general. Very much like George Washington, Greene's studying of war tactics as a young man taught him not to be bold, but certain when engaging with the enemy, which is a trait that he carried with him from the start to the end of his command of the southern campaigns. This discipline meant that sometimes Greene anticipated the worst and imagined threats that were not present. Marion felt that this was the case and that Greene was sending Marion's men all over the place just to reassure himself that the British were not escaping. For two weeks in August 1782, Greene ordered Marion to be in constant motion around the perimeter of Charleston. These movements produced minor skirmishes with the British in which Marion reported two killed and three wounded.[107]

Greene was still having major supply problems and sometimes had to send his troops out with four rounds per man. Because they were careful not to waste any ammunition, sometimes they had to let British foraging parties move past.[108] The shortage of troops gave Greene reason to panic, as he received word that the British were receiving five thousand men as reinforcements in Charleston. Greene wrote to Colonel Lee, "Col Laurens wrote me last night that by good intelligence from Charles Town he had great reason to believe a large reinforcement was on their passage from New York and within a day or two sail of Charles Town. Should the report be true we shall have the devil to pay."[109]

This was everything that Greene feared would happen and a reminder of how volatile and dangerous the military situation remained in 1782. The British would have nearly eight thousand men in Charleston and could easily overwhelm the dwindling Patriot numbers stationed outside the city. He figured that while peace negotiations went on in Europe, the British were bargaining for a stronger position and would have it if they held parts of the South.

He desperately wrote for reinforcements but received only a response from Washington later saying that he felt that there was a threat of invasion in Virginia and he could not afford to send any men.[110] Greene did not agree and still argued that freeing Charleston was the key to pushing the British out of the South. After abandoning their key holding, they were sure to remove troops from the Carolinas and Georgia Lowcountry. Luckily, word came in that this reinforcement the British was receiving only consisted of five hundred men. "Still, with the weakness of the Patriot army," Conrad wrote, "Greene wrote to Lee that the entire episode left him 'confoundedly alarmed' and he still needed to secure more men and supplies for his army."[111] Greene became a political force in South Carolina to try to rectify this situation.

One of Greene's major tasks in 1782 was assisting in the rebuilding of civil government. Once Greene had removed the British from the upcountry, he wrote to Governor Rutledge in May 1781 asking him to return to South Carolina and organize elections.[112] Greene wanted to have a sitting legislature in South Carolina to show that they would not remain under control of the British and to improve the Americans' position with negotiations going on in Paris. Like Washington, Greene was careful never to usurp civilian control, but he was a strong voice in the state as the military commander.

Additionally, Greene wanted South Carolinians to believe that they would have law and order in the state with a government to stop the plundering and lawless behavior. A widow from the prominent Wragg family of Charleston wrote to Greene, "I have been plundered continually by militia parties at my plantations. Please provide protection and redress as I have been informed that it is not your wish to have private property hurt."[113]

Greene found the general social disorder in the state extremely distasteful and was determined to bring about an established government. Rutledge agreed that elections were necessary but felt that he could not do anything until those exiled returned to Charleston.

Those exiled included the conservative Charleston gentry who had previously held positions in the government. Without their influence, the government would be controlled by representatives from the upcountry and, therefore, not balanced. Greene found the governor to have sound reasons to wait. However, he was determined to stop the lawlessness going on in the state.

In the absence of Rutledge, the army was acting as the law enforcement to stop excessive plundering like what had happened at the Wragg plantation.[114] Greene made many executive decisions for South Carolina as commander of the military in the absence of the Charleston diplomats but was happy to turn over his unofficial authority to elected representatives on January 8, 1782.[115]

Many military leaders had seats in the new legislature, and Greene's influence was still significant. Some of the state's commanders with seats were Marion, Sumter, Hampton and Horry. The legislature met just thirty-six miles from Charleston in Jacksonboro, provisional capital of South Carolina, which was chosen so that the government's presence would show the British that they controlled almost the entire state. This legislative authority would help the Americans' position while negotiating in Paris and put pressure on the British to leave Charleston.

Chapter 6

"YOU KNOW ME TOO WELL TO SUPPOSE I SHALL SHRINK AT SMALL DIFFICULTIES"

I will do all I can and you know me too well to suppose I shall shrink at small difficulties, but how feeble are the best intentions, and how vain an obstinate perseverance against a very unequal force.

—Greene to George Washington on his struggles in 1782

Greene was pleased with the status of the South Carolina Assembly for now, so he returned back to the issue of needing more troop strength. While Greene was dealing with political issues, there were still skirmishes happening all over Charleston. On January 11, 1782, Greene carried out a mission to push the British out of Johns Island. He described the event in a letter to Rutledge explaining that the endeavor ended successfully in that "the enemy retreated to James Island leaving behind some few stores and destroying some others."[116] However, there were some obstacles along the way, as the tides prevented the men from crossing the river at certain times and the British had gunboats guarding a pass. Like most of Greene's victories, things did not go as planned, but the end result was favorable. It was clear, though, that he needed more men if he was going to keep up a strong Patriot force in the face of a massive British army. Greene proposed a solution of using slaves to fight the enemy to Washington. It was not new, as the British had already been doing this. He wrote:

> *I have recommended to this State to raise some black Regiments. To fill up their regiments with whites is impracticable and to get reinforcements from the Northwards precarious, and at best difficult, from the prejudices respecting the climate. Some are for it, but the far greater part of the people are opposed to it.*[117]

South Carolinians already saw the British using slaves in their lines and felt that this made them weak, which further contributed to Greene's problems concerning public opinion: "John Laurens sent Greene intelligence from Charleston indicating that a committee of diehard Loyalists planned to ask for more arms and ammunition for the defense of Charlestown which they planned to undertake with the help of the negroes. Laurens commented that the plan 'resembles the desperate unavailing efforts of a drowning man.'"[118] The public scoffed at the use of slaves and became overly hostile toward black British units such as the Black Dragoons.

South Carolinians had exercised benevolent paternalism toward the slaves as their masters and felt that their relationship had turned into that of an obstinate son disobeying his father. Some soldiers relished the opportunity to confront the black soldiers, smugly reporting that they "sliced and dissected" some of the Black Dragoons.[119] Most Patriots dismissed the freed slaves as soldiers because they had no knowledge of military skills or how to use weapons. Greene did not underestimate a perfectly capable source of manpower to solve a problem he had been having during his entire command of the southern campaigns. He thought that perhaps he could copy the British on this matter. It was clear to him that he would not be receiving reinforcement from Congress, and the northerners were complaining about serving in the southern heat. "A plan was written to purchase 3,000 blacks at $1,000 each to fight for the Patriots but it was never executed. South Carolina balked at the institution of the plan, contending that a precedent would be set for the British, which might well end in the destructions of Southern agriculture."[120]

Southerners were not scared of their slaves taking up arms against them but were fearful of what would become of their farms with no labor source. For most of the war, Patriots had been terrified of British efforts to recruit their slaves. One of the most surprising revelations from Greene's papers is the degree to which Patriots in 1781 and 1782 looked on such British efforts as desperate and nonthreatening. They also knew that many slaves were not rushing to sign up to fight with the British during this time. Frey explained, "The surpassing cruelty that was the hallmark of the war in South Carolina

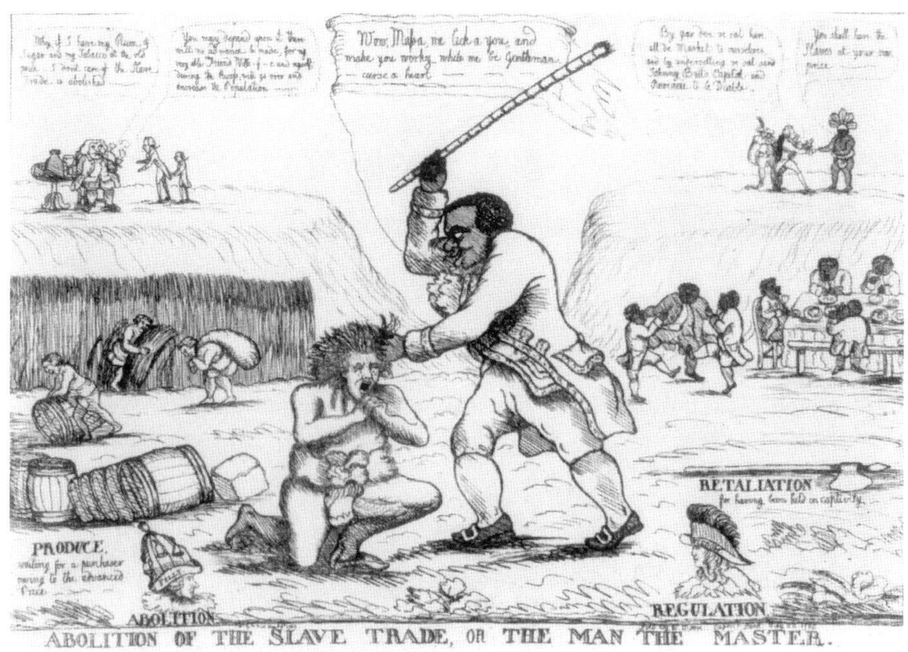

British political cartoon depicting former slaves taking revenge on masters. British officers promised freedom to slaves who fought against the Americans. Published in 1789. *Courtesy of Library of Congress.*

constituted a compelling reason why many slaves viewed the British offer of freedom with caution. Severe punishment, and often death, was a virtual certainty for an unsuccessful escape. Thousands of slaves stayed on the farms and plantations."[121] South Carolinians had been fearful of slaves revolting in the past, but they were less concerned with revolts in this period and did not want to free their own slaves who were not attempting to escape.

Additionally, others had their eyes set on using slaves to further their personal situations. Massey argued, "In 1782 enterprising backcountry farmers recognized that ownership of slaves fulfilled their dreams of accumulating more wealth."[122] The vast majority of the House members shared the viewpoint of the public and were not planning to give up their own slaves to a fighting force. The British promised the slaves freedom in exchange for fighting, but Americans were unwilling to make that promise. Laurens, who had initially thought the Loyalists recruiting slaves to help was laughable, admired Greene's resourcefulness and thought he might be suggesting that the blacks who fought be given their freedom when treated as soldiers. Laurens was one of the few who held this viewpoint, as most

Patriots did not see the slaves as a skilled military force and needed their labor on their farms.

Greene had written to Rutledge previously asking to use some of the enslaved for his army,[123] but most likely his need for reinforcements surpassed his humanitarian concern for the enslaved. Some men in the army were becoming upset over the treatment of the slaves and aware of the cruel irony of the Patriots fighting for their own rights and liberties while they denied the blacks their own. They chose not to dwell on the fact that many of their slaves had seen the British army as the real agent of freedom.[124] Greene continuously preached the practical necessity of using the slaves to fight, and Laurens supported the idea in the Privy Council. Unfortunately, this was not the answer to Greene's prayer for more men, as the proposal was soundly defeated. By March, Greene was desperately short of troops and supplies for the troops he did have. He wrote to Washington:

> *We have 300 men now without arms, and twice that number so naked as to be unfit for any duty but in cases of desperation. Men and officers without pay in this situation cannot be kept in temper long. I will not trouble you with a detail of all of our difficulties. I persuaded the legislature to raise black regiments but could not prevail. All the southern states look to you for support. I will do all I can and you know me to well to suppose I shall shrink at small difficulties.*[125]

Greene had everything against him in 1782, and he could not mask the problem much longer.

Greene had been using deceptive tactics to cover the fact that he had a weak army by constantly moving his men around Charleston and plundering to obtain food and clothing. Now that the plundering had finally come to an end and no provisions were being sent, Greene paid his men himself. He also reported that while his training of his army was making the men more effective to make up for the numbers, their terms of service were expiring, and he was not getting replacements. The situation should have been resolved by now, as settlement was imminent in Paris and the British were willing to abandon the offensive. However, there was a mutual distrust between the British and Americans in Charleston due to past actions like the Americans burning a British hospital on the Cooper River[126] and the execution of Patriot hero Isaac Hayne.[127]

Hayne became a martyr for the Patriot cause, as he had been an active revolutionary and somewhat of a hero. When Charleston fell in 1780,

Hayne was paroled to his plantation. The British authorities later asked him to fight for their cause, and Hayne took this to mean he was free of his parole. So, as a true Patriot, he rejoined the militia as a commander of a regiment just south of Charleston. During a raid near the city, Hayne's unit was overtaken, and he was captured. The British viewed Hayne as a traitor and tried him for treason. He was hanged on August 4, 1781, without the chance to appeal the verdict.

The Americans were completely outraged; Greene's camp was particularly angry and wanted revenge on the Loyalists. Greene had to keep the men under control because he did not want the situation in Charleston to get worse for the Americans. He wrote a letter to the British commander in Charleston, Nisbet Balfour, expressing his outrage and questioning the execution: "I am informed of a flagrant violation in the cruel and unjust execution of Col Hanes [*sic*] for which I mean an immediate retaliation unless you can offer some thing more to justify the measure than I am informed of or is mentioned in the Charles Town paper."[128] Greene never did retaliate for the murder of Isaac Hayne but would threaten to do so if there were more unjust hangings.

The militia would remember Isaac Hayne and fight hard in his memory for months to come. The men would not soon forget their feelings of mistrust toward the British, and these sentiments carried into 1782. The bloodshed continued in small skirmishes on the outskirts of Charleston. Colonel Horry wrote to Greene on February 28, 1782, of a conflict that resulted in a few deaths. He wrote that the enemy surprised Marion and his own unit, camping at Wambaw on Johns Island.[129] Their purpose was to obtain fresh meat, and they succeeded—much to the disgrace of Marion, who lost eight men with several wounded, while Horry lost twelve, including two officers. Significantly, many of the American militiamen in this skirmish were redeemed Loyalists.

Another reason why violence continued in the last stages of the war in South Carolina was the Patriot state government's treatment of the Loyalists in 1782. Greene had continued to favor Washington's advocacy of moderation for the Loyalists, as he saw no other way for them to live peacefully after the war if the Loyalists were not reconciled and incorporated into postwar society. This was not the popular opinion, as most Patriots were calling for revenge, and many Tories left Charleston because of this animosity.

Governor Rutledge was having a hard time trying to find a way to deal with the Loyalists, and even he wanted to deny them the right to rejoin the state as citizens.[130] He did not trust that they would be sincere in supporting the new country even if they joined as citizens. Others agreed and felt that the country could not move completely forward with Loyalists, so removing them and seizing their lands, property and slaves would solve many problems for the new government of South Carolina.

Greene was not worried about this and had many reasons to support a moderate policy toward the Loyalists. He felt that if forgiveness was not extended to the Loyalists, they might not leave and take up arms with the British to protect themselves. Greene also thought the Loyalists could provide a solution to the lack of men for his army. If using black slaves was not an option, he figured pardon could be granted to Tories if they fought with Greene against the British.[131] The offer of citizenship could be what they needed to join, and some of the provisions they were providing the British in Charleston could be given to the Patriot army.

He also noticed that his own militia seemed to be targeting Loyalists in their plundering. Greene thought that the government declaring them to be the enemy of the state was not helping curb the excessive plundering that he so detested. He wrote, "Plundering is destructive to the moral and manners of a people."[132] Creating a policy of leniency toward the Loyalists could get more men for Greene's army; provide more food, clothing and ammunition; and stop thefts. Greene, like Washington, also thought this was the right thing to do to move forward and create civilization in South Carolina.

Rutledge finally agreed with Greene and decided that any Loyalist who signed up within a month and served for six months would receive a pardon. Conrad clarified, "Some classes of the more obnoxious Loyalists such as those who held civil or military commissions as of September 27, 1781, were excluded."[133] Greene was extremely pleased with this policy, and it drew in a number of Tories to fight with Marion. However, for those "obnoxious" Loyalists, options were limited.

Another new policy stated that Loyalists who did not cooperate would have their property seized or worse. Jasanoff clarified, "Confiscation acts passed by the South Carolina Patriot legislature in 1782 expelled some five hundred prominent Loyalists as traitors on pain of death, taking their property, and subjecting those who 'traiterously assist abet and participate in treasonable practices' to similar penalties.'"[134] Almost four hundred Tories would have their land taken when the bill passed successfully. Revenge was the main reason this measure was taken, although the money gained from this would help South Carolina have a more stable financial future. Greene was most displeased with the bill but never said anything publicly about

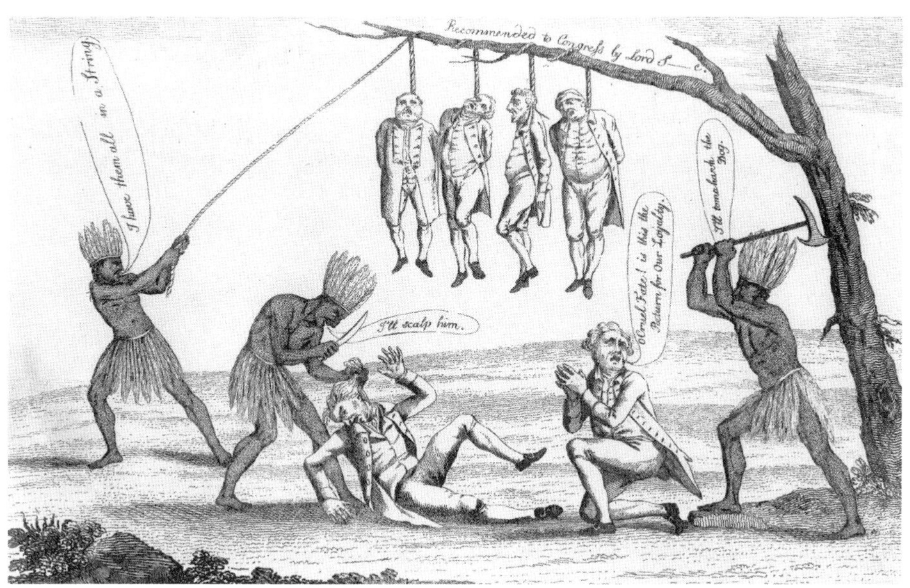

British political cartoon depicting the fate of Loyalists at the hands of three natives, representing America. Sold by W. Humphrey in March 1783. *Courtesy of Library of Congress.*

it.[135] However, he would have later difficulties with political leaders in South Carolina because of his views.

The British were obviously not pleased with the new measures the Patriots had taken, so in the late spring of 1782, they threatened to seize the slaves of Patriots and force them to fight against their masters.[136] These turned out to be empty threats, and the Loyalists who were not pardoned had no option but to leave South Carolina. The country was coming out of a civil war, and most likely the Loyalists had no home to return to, as their property had probably been seized or destroyed in their absence. There were British ships offering free passage, and "Loyalists who left would enjoy the security of remaining in the British Empire."[137]

The majority of Loyalist civilians in Charleston made up their minds to go. While northern Loyalist refugees traveled to Nova Scotia or Britain, southern Loyalists wished to keep the slaves they still had; those two areas did not allow for slavery. "Jamaica and other British West Indian islands seemed a better option, but these well-settled islands had little uncultivated land available, and were known for their high cost of living and high chance of dying of tropical disease."[138] The only British territory left for southern slave owners to live was east Florida, and they went in droves.

As the end of British occupation drew near, the newly minted Major General Alexander Leslie wished to end the fighting and negotiate a truce of sorts with the Americans. Leslie had replaced Cornwallis as commander of the South in 1782. Greene, however, did not trust the British and insisted that only total surrender would end the fighting.[139] The British army was not engaging with the Americans on purpose; they only plundered and foraged to look for provisions for themselves. But Greene resisted those foraging expeditions to the end, and in one of these foraging skirmishes, Colonel John Laurens was killed.

One of the larger fights in 1782, this skirmish became known as the Battle of Combahee River. Because Greene refused the truce, Leslie threatened that his army would take what it needed from the Charleston area. On August 27, British expeditions went up the Combahee River outside Beaufort. Greene heard of these movements and sent Laurens and General Mordecai Gist of Maryland to deal with them. Unfortunately, the British anticipated the Americans' pursuit and set up an ambush to meet them. Laurens fell in this ambush, and the British held their ground, obtaining their provisions and sailing back to Charleston. Greene was devastated by the loss and wrote, "The army has lost a brave officer and the public a worthy citizen."[140] Washington and Alexander Hamilton felt similarly about the loss of Laurens, viewing the young officer's death as a highly significant moment in the last months of the war. It was regrettable that he lost his life in such a little skirmish over cattle and barrels of rice, but this conflict demonstrated that the British were still inflicting harm.[141]

Despite skirmishes with the British in 1782 and after Greene had forced the British into the greater Charleston area in December 1781, the army did not have much to do. The few men he did have were sickly, restless and dwelled on their problems. Greene's army threated to mutiny and ravage locals for provisions. His officers even bickered among themselves over rank. Morale was low, and Greene felt like he was acting as a referee and therapist.[142] Luckily, Greene was able to keep the army together enough with the addition of Loyalists and the use of superb cavalry deception tactics. In this way, he could apply enough pressure on the British in Charleston. His army occasionally engaged with the British in small skirmishes, keeping them on the defensive and from expanding into the country. The addition of the new state government sitting just outside Charleston also sent out the message that the Americans were capable of leading and forcing the British to leave. For months, Greene had been preparing for this momentous occasion. He just did not know when this would happen. He wrote to Lee:

> *Our Army has been exceedingly sickly this Campaign, much more so than they were the last. Indeed our sick list far out numbered our well Men; and the Mortality in the months of August and September have been great. I hope soon to have this Country free from the enemy, every preparation is making for the evacuation of Charles Town. The refugees are already sailed for St Augustine.*[143]

Greene's hope would come true, and his preparations would not be in vain. The British threat of retaliation never materialized, and finally, British commander Leslie received official orders to evacuate Charleston in October 1782. These orders meant that the British were to end any and all offensive actions and prepare to leave. Richard Henry Lee learned of the news and wrote immediately to Greene from his home in Virginia:

> *I am happy in so good an opportunity as Capt Carnes presents for paying my respects to you which I should much oftener do if safe conveyances more frequently offered. We are here induced to hope the enemy will leave you nothing more to do in the south by their evacuation of Charlestown in the course of this month. The South must long remember your services and be grateful for them. The last account from England informs us that the negotiation was still going on, but that little effect was expected from it as the King was obstinate and had a Ministry to his mind. I am much mistaken if the necessity of the case does not soon compel the British King to grin and grant independence to America.*[144]

Lee most likely was aware of the intense negotiations that had been going on in London and the threat of *uti possidetis.* By October, though, it seemed that everything was working in the Americans' favor and the king was just being obstinate and trying to save some of his dignity. He would have to recall his troops and give his former colonies their independence. Now the cause for the uncertainty was over when the British would actually leave Charleston.

Greene began to make preparations for the evacuation in November. He wrote to many leaders asking what he should do and giving status reports to them. He was based in Ashley Hill near present-day Goose Creek. He wrote to Governor John Mathews of South Carolina:

> *Your favor of yesterday is before* [me] *respecting the mode of taking possession of Charles Town and I have to inform you that should the*

Dear Sir, Chantilly October the 5th 1782

I am happy in so good an opportunity as Capt. Carnes presents for paying my respects to you which I should much oftener do if safe conveyances were more frequently offered. We are here induced to hope that the enemy will leave you nothing more to do in the south by their evacuation of Charles Town in the course of this month. You will then have the glory of commencing, prosecuting, and effecting the recovery of a great part of this union from the grasp of Tyranny and oppression. The South must long remember your services and be grateful for them. It is the conjecture of many that New York will also be evacuated – but I fear that adversity hath not yet sufficiently chastened the Tyrants mind to produce such a total giving up of N. America as the quitting N. York would imply. This idea seems to be strongly suggested by the parliamentary debates upon the resignation of Mr. Fox, which leaves no room to doubt about the fixt determination not to yield the independence of these States but to the most invincible necessity. The last account from England informs us that the negotiation was still going on, but that little effect was expected from it as the King was obstinate and

Above: First page of correspondence from Richard Henry Lee to Nathanael Greene, dated October 5, 1782. Lee expresses negotiations in London and thoughts that the British will leave Charleston soon. *American Revolutionary War Papers of the Charleston Museum Archives.*

and had a Ministry to his mind. But tho the King be obstinate and has a ministry to his mind, and altho N. York be not speedily quitted, I am much mistaken if the necessity of the case [illegible] compel the British King to grin & grant independence to America. A fine Lesson this for Tyrants who may learn from hence that evil deeds may force with convulsive pangs from the tortured soul, that which it most abhors to grant. Gen. Washington is now at the head of 17,000 men well appointed and well disciplined, so that we are in a good posture to meet whatever turn affairs may take.

Accept, if you please, my best wishes for your health and prosperity, for I am with great sincerity and affectionate esteem Sir your most obedient and very humble servant

Richard Henry Lee

Right: Reverse page of correspondence from Richard Henry Lee to Greene, dated October 5, 1782. *American Revolutionary War Papers of the Charleston Museum Archives.*

> *enemy evacuate the place your wishes shall be carried into execution as far as possible should no maneuvers of the Enemy render other measures necessary. I wish your Excellency to be prepared to follow the Troops as early as you can render it convenient. When you are ready to enter the Town if you will be so obliging as to let me know it I will order a party of horse to conduct you.*[145]

Greene and Mathews both expected that the British would be leaving soon and that the evacuation would be quick.

The announcement had come in October, but they would not leave until mid-December. This uncertainty kept Greene on his toes because his army could not leave until the British did. He wrote to one of his officers, "From the great uncertainty of the enemy's evacuating Charlestown this winter if at all I am induced to halt your troops until I can satisfy myself more fully of their intentions. If they don't evacuate in a few days I shall be pretty fully convinced they don't mean to this winter, and therefore it will be unsafe and improper for your troops to go home."[146] Greene and others were in a constant state of suspense over whether the British were going to be leaving this winter or not.

Everyone thought that it might not even happen until much later. Greene had to write to Marion as well with instructions for the militia in regards to the evacuation for whenever that was to happen:

> *For fear the Militia with you may imagine they are kept out of Town should the enemy leave at the instance of the Army, I have sent you a copy of the Governors letter on the subject. As there will be a variety of charactors in Charles Town and as the officers of the Army are strangers to the whole I shall be obliged to you with three or four of your particular friends to enter the Town with the party that takes possession or as soon after as possible and remain there until the Governor arrives. The Country Militia you may dismiss the moment you are informed the Town is evacuated. But at present I am at a loss to tell how or when that is to happen.*[147]

While Greene was making plans for the eventual evacuation, he was still dealing with keeping his army fed, clothed and together. The militiamen were ready to be finished with their service, but Greene had to have them stay with Marion until he got the news.

With the British forced into Charleston, Greene and his men only had to stop them and his own men from raiding nearby homes. When the town would actually be evacuated was an uncertainty that Greene was tired of dealing with as a commander. But finally, on December 14, transports arrived to take the British out of Charleston for good. That morning, Greene and the light infantry were the first troops to march into town. In the afternoon, Greene accompanied the governor and other governmental officials to parade in triumph down the streets.[118] Greene also helped establish a police force to take over the job of patrolling the town from the military. Greene was pleased to report that the civilians took over the city the next day. Charleston was finally liberated and open for business as usual. General William Moultrie was present that day and recorded the most complete report on the events of December 14, 1782, which follows here in full:

EVACUATION.

On Saturday, the fourteenth day of December, 1782, the British troops evacuated Charlestown, after having possession two years, seven months, and two days.

The evacuation took place in the following manner: Brigadier General Wayne was ordered to cross the Ashley River, with three hundred light infantry, eighty of Lee's cavalry, and twenty artillery, with two six pounders, to move down towards the British lines, which was near Colonel Shubrick's, and consisted of three redoubts. General Leslie, who commanded in town, sent a message to General Wayne, informing him that he would next day leave the town, and for the peace and security of the inhabitants, and of the town, would propose to leave their advanced works next day at the firing of the morning gun; at which time General Wayne should move on slowly, and take possession; and from thence to follow the british troops into town, keeping at a respectful distance (say about two hundred yards) and when the British troops, after passing through the town gates, should file off to Gadsden's wharf, General Wayne was to proceed into town, which was done with great order and regularity, except now and then the British called to General Wayne that he was too fast upon them, which occasioned him to halt a little. About 11 o'clock, A.M. the American troops marched into town and took post at the state-house.

At 3 o'clock, P.M. General Greene conducted governor Mathews, and the Council, with some others of the citizens into town; we marched in, in the following order: an advance of an officer of thirty of Lee's dragoons; then followed the governor and General Greene, the next two were General Gist and myself, after us followed the council, citizens and officers, making

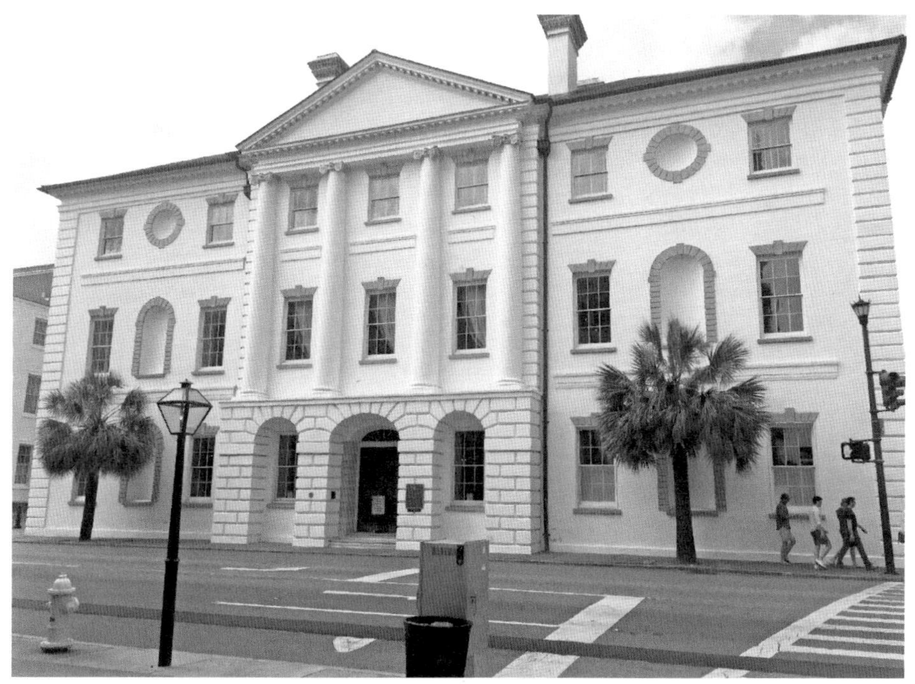

Present-day Charleston County Courthouse, originally built in 1753 as South Carolina's first and only colonial statehouse. It was used as the central meeting place for South Carolina politics. *Photo by author.*

altogether about fifty; one hundred and eighty cavalry brought up the rear; we halted in Broad street, opposite where the South Carolina bank now stands, there we alighted, and the cavalry discharged to quarters: afterwards, every one went where they pleased; some in viewing the town, others in visiting their friends. It was a grand and pleasing sight to see the enemy's fleet (upwards of three hundred sail) laying at anchor from Fort Johnson to Five fathom-hole, in a curve line, as the current runs, and what made it more agreeable, they were ready to depart from the port. The great joy that was felt on this day, by the citizens and soldiers, was inexpressible: the windows, the orphans, the aged men and others, who, from their particular situations, were obliged to remain in Charlestown, many of whom had been cooped up in one room of their own elegant houses for upwards of two years, whilst the other parts were occupied by the British officers, many of whom were a rude uncivil set of gentlemen; their situations, and the many mortifying circumstances occurred to them in that time, must have been truly distressing. I cannot forget that happy day when we marched into

Charleston with the American troops: it was a proud day to me, and I felt myself much elated, at seeing the balconies, the doors and windows crowded with the Patriotic fair, and aged citizens and others, congratulating us on our return home, saying, "God bless you, gentlemen! You are welcome home, gentlemen!" Both citizens and soldiers shed mutual tears of joy.

It was an ample reward for the triumphant soldier, after all the hazards and fatigues of war, which he had gone through, to be the instrument of

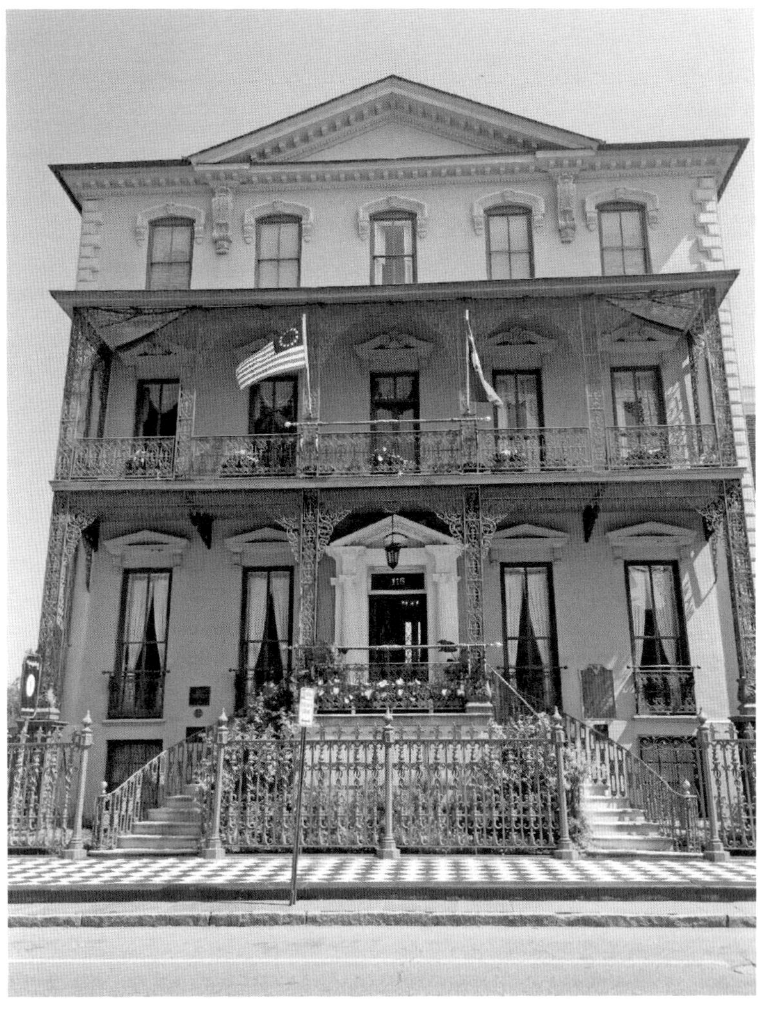

Located on Broad Street, the John Rutledge House was Nathanael Greene's headquarters in Charleston. It is presently a bed-and-breakfast but was the home of John Rutledge, the first governor of South Carolina. *Photo by author.*

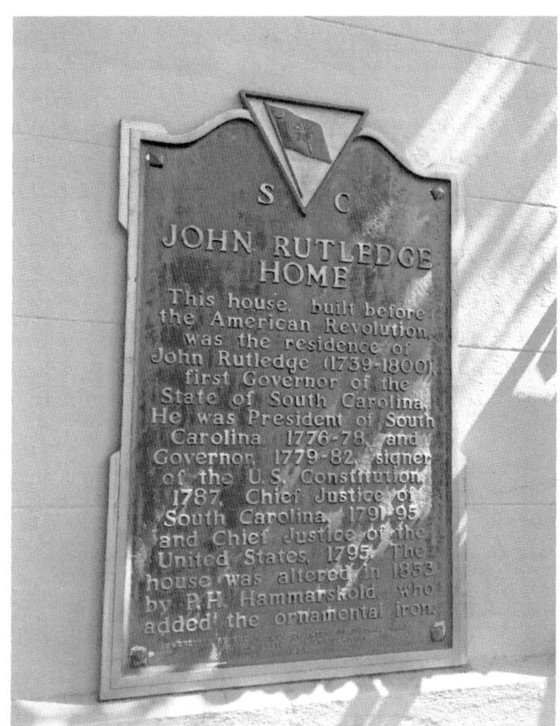

Right: Historic marker on exterior of the inn. *Photo by author.*

Below: Interior shot of the ballroom of the John Rutledge House. It is called the "Signer's Ballroom," as Rutledge wrote drafts of the U.S. Constitution in this room. *Photo by author.*

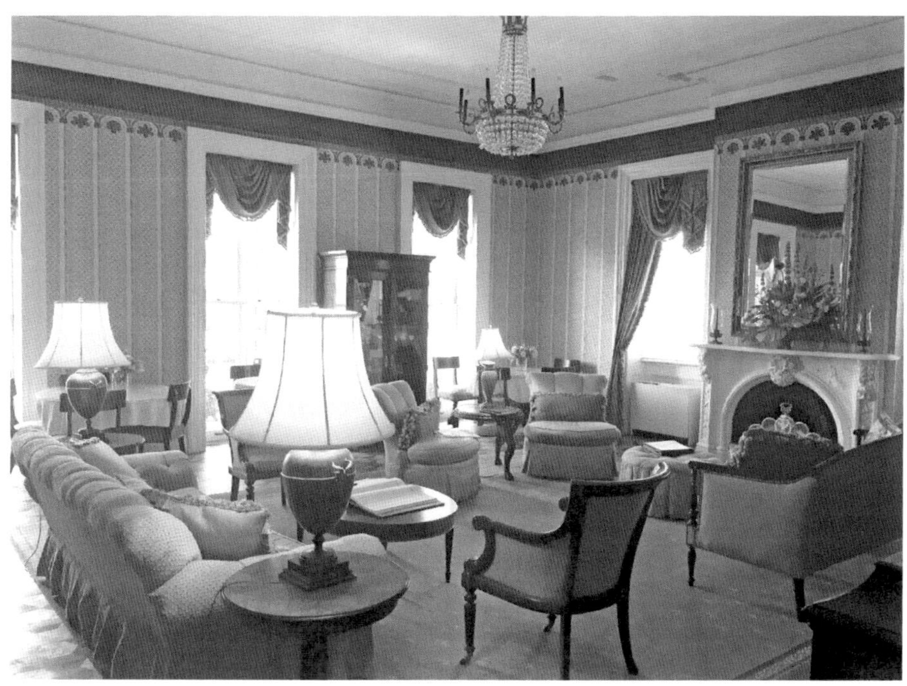

> *releasing his friends and fellow citizens from captivity, and restoring to them their liberties and possession of their city and country again.*
>
> *This fourteenth day of December, 1782, ought never to be forgotten by the Carolinians; it ought to be a day of festivity with them, and it was the real day of their deliverance and independence.*[149]

General Moultrie was present at the evacuation and enjoyed the events of the day. This account was not published until 1802, and he was well advanced in his years by that time. He was known for his humanity, honor and consideration for all of his fellow Charlestonians, whether Whig or Tory.

Greene wasted no time to send word of the joyous occasion out to every major national player. His accounts of the events of December 14 are not as detailed as Moultrie's account, but one letter has Greene's thoughts recorded more so than others. On December 19, Greene wrote from his new Charleston headquarters to the president of the Continental Congress, Elias Boudinot:

> *I have the honor to communicate to your Excellency the agreeable information of the evacuation of Charles Town, and beg leave to congratulate you upon the event. The enemy compleated their embarkation on the 14th, and the same day fell down into Rebellion Road, and on the seventeenth crossed the Bar and went to sea.*
>
> *Knowing the impossibility of doing the Enemy any material injury on their embarkation in a fortified Town, and under cover of their shipping; and being well informed that some attempts had been made by some of the Refugee followers of the British Army, to fire the place, I directed the General to make the safety of the Town first object. The conditions being understood by both parties, the Town was evacuated and possessed without the least confusion, our advance following close up the Rear. The Governor was conducted into his Capital the same Day, the civil police established the day following, and the Day after the Town opened for business.*
>
> *This important event gives us compleat possession of all Southern States; and what adds to its consequence, I had the happiness to negociate a few Weeks ago a general Exchange of all the Civil and Militia Officers, as well as privates of every denomination under military paroles, belonging to the Southern department.*
>
> *The People are once more free, and I hope will manifest their gratitude by a vigorous exertion in support of the common Cause. The struggle and*

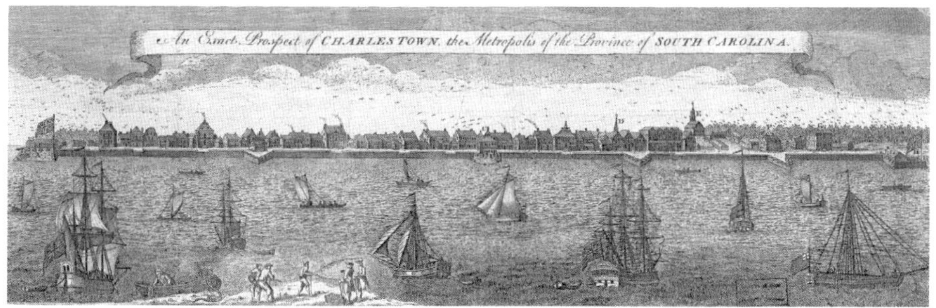

Waterfront view of Charleston Harbor, engraved in 1762 *London Miagazine*. *Courtesy of Library of Congress.*

> *conflict has been long and severe; but when it is considered that the Enemy had upwards of 18,000 regular Troops, besides several thousands Militia and Negroes employed for the reduction of the Southern States, I hope it will be found that the progress of the Southern Army, has been no less honorable than important; and that it will merit the approbation of Congress through every stage of the operations.*
>
> *I should be wanting in gratitude to the Army was I to omit expressing my warmest acknowledgements for the zeal and activity with which they attempted and persevered in every enterprise, and for the patience and dignity with which they bore their sufferings. Perhaps no Army ever exhibited greater proofs of Patriotism and public virtue. It has been my constant care to alleviate their distresses as much as possible, but my endeavors have been far short of my wishes, or their merit.*

It had been a long two years for Greene; he fought a number of battles all over the state, dealt with problems of supplies and manpower the entire time and fought with not only the British and their allies but also state politicians. Charleston cannot thank Nathanael Greene enough for his efforts, especially in the period following Eutaw Springs until the end of 1782. During this year, there was apathy, an assumption of victory, a few skirmishes, dwindling Patriot troops and political controversy. The British continued to hold Charleston as a diplomatic bargaining chip. But it was Nathanael Greene's decisions and strategies that held the Continental army together and ultimately led to his triumphal liberation of Charleston.

EPILOGUE

It had been happy for me if I could have lived a private life in peace and plenty, enjoying all the happiness that results from a well-tempered society founded on mutual esteem. But the injury done my country, and the chains of slavery forging for all posterity, called me forth to defend our common rights, and repel the bold invaders of the sons of freedom.

—Greene reflecting on the war

Greene successfully removed the British from Charleston after fighting with them for two years. December 14, 1782, was a joyous occasion for Greene, as he was able to march down the streets in triumph, but the war did not end there. If the recapture of Charleston had ended the war, Greene would have finished his service as a hero, and his relationship with South Carolina would have ended on good terms. Unfortunately, Greene still had to keep together his demoralized army for seven more months, until the Treaty of Paris was officially concluded in 1783, and try to get supplies from the government. He still faced remaining British armies in the South Carolina Lowcountry. Greene was deeply involved in the politics of South Carolina, requesting provisions and encouraging the growth of an effective central government. He had been happy to turn over his unofficial authority of civil matters in the absence of the South Carolina diplomats but still wanted to offer his opinions and assist where needed.

While Greene's goals remained unchanged, popular opinion of him had changed. Many Carolinians stopped seeing Greene as a statesman committed to making the future of the state better but rather as a meddling nuisance. He particularly had difficulties with the new governor, Benjamin Guerard. His support of the arming of blacks and policy of moderation for the Loyalists made him many enemies.[150] As the British had withdrawn from Charleston, there was no longer a need for the Continental army to be as involved in the governing of South Carolina. Traditional fears of the presence of a standing army began to reemerge. Furthermore, South Carolinians were upset that they alone seemed to bear the burden of the entire war in the South. They did not want any measures to be taken to complicate their lives any further.

At the end of 1782, South Carolina officials ordered the end of impressment, which compromised Greene's ability to maintain the army in 1783.[151] The Continental army had been habitually taking what it needed for public service, and without the supplies it gained from this, Greene had to think of other options. Additionally, there was a change in the government of South Carolina, as Henry Laurens and John Rutledge were dropped from the congressional delegation. Both of those men were strong nationalists who sided with Greene on most issues. The delegation now consisted of Ralph Izard, Jacob Reed and Thomas Sumter, all of whom opposed a strong government. "Predictably," Conrad quipped, "Greene, as the nation's most visible agent, became a scapegoat."[152] Greene was not fazed, as he continued to stress the importance of a national government. In a letter to Governor Guerard, Greene wrote:

> *I am one of those who think our independence can only prove a blessing under congressional influence. That if we have anything to apprehend, it is, that the members of congress will sacrifice the general interest to particular interests in the state to which they belong; that this is the case, and from the very nature and constitution of that body, more was to be dreaded from their exercising too little than too much power.*[153]

Guerard did not agree with Greene, and the two had further problems. Greene gave a British officer a flag of truce to visit Charleston on private business. Guerard ignored Greene's pass and arrested the British officer and his party. This arrest had the potential to become a crisis, and Greene ordered that the men be released on grounds that this was a military matter. He was furious and even threatened military action against Guerard.[154] The governor did back down and released the men but stated that they needed to leave Charleston quickly. While this is a small issue, it demonstrates the hostility of many toward the British and Greene's job of advocating for peace moving forward.

In the last few months of his command, Greene still tried to steer South Carolina toward support of the national government. However, he met hesitation and opposition at every turn and ultimately failed. He became angry and frustrated, attempting to tell the southern leaders to respect government and the army. Finally, in April, news of peace arrived, and the Continental troops were no longer needed. The army that had reconquered South Carolina was finally disbanded and went home in July. After a long two and a half years in the South, Greene left for Rhode Island on August 11, 1783. Greene's political views had become increasingly unpopular, but just as every single one of Greene's military defeats had actually helped the Americans in the long run, the same was true for his public policies. His advocacy of a strong national government did eventually lead to the emergence of a strong Federalist faction in the lower South.

The leaders of the Continental army were especially prominent among the Federalists, while the militia favored local or state control. It became a contest between Greene's supporters and Thomas Sumter's. However, that is not a debate that Greene continued to play a role in moving forward. After returning to Rhode Island, he and his family moved down to Georgia to live in Mulberry Grove plantation, and he made this home his permanent residence. Unfortunately, the rest of Greene's life was marked by financial difficulty, as he struggled to make his plantation into a working one and fell deep into debt.[155] While he was at war, Greene's family members had mismanaged his funds, and the establishment of Mulberry Grove and his second plantation left him in bad shape. South Carolina and Georgia had ample gratitude for Greene's command and contributions to those states, so they had rewarded him with these plantations. However, his financial situation had gotten even worse when creditors held him personally responsible for hiring a company to help him obtain supplies for his troops. In the middle of trying to figure out his financial hardships, Greene died suddenly of sunstroke in June 1786.

The South was deprived of a strong commander who was important in advocating for a national government. We cannot know if Greene would have gone on to be the leader of the South in the new republic, but we can assume that based on his leadership ability and success in the military, he would have had an important role. We can also say that Greene would probably have been a household name like many of his contemporaries. Although many do not know the extent to which they owe Greene, he has at

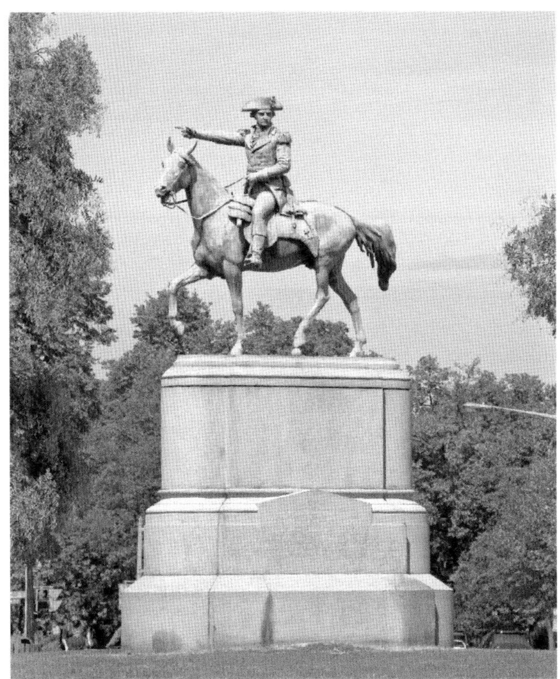

Left: Statue of American Revolutionary War Major General Nathanael Greene in Stanton Park, Washington, D.C. George F. Landegger Collection of District of Columbia Photographs in Carol M. Highsmith's America. *Courtesy of Library of Congress.*

Below: Poem about Greenville engraved in marble underneath statue of Nathanael Greene in Greenville, South Carolina. *Photo by author.*

GREENVILLE'S GENERAL

HAVE YOU HEARD THE STORY OF GENERAL GREENE
A RHODE ISLAND PRIVATE WHO FOLLOWED HIS DREAM
IN 1780 AS WASHINGTON'S MAN
HE CAME TO OUR STATE TO FREE OUR GREAT LAND

ARMIES OF BRITISH WERE SENT BY THE KING
BUT THEY WERE NO MATCH FOR THE GENIUS OF GREENE
BACKED BY THE BRAVEST OF ILL-EQUIPPED MEN
THE PATRIOTS FOUGHT TO THE GLORIOUS END

THERE WERE PICKENS AND SUMTER AND MARION TOO
WILD MEN AT HEART BUT TO GREENE THEY WERE TRUE
THESE GHOSTS OF THE WOODLANDS WHO TOOK UP THE CAUSE
GAVE THE REDCOATS AND INDIANS A REASON TO PAUSE

FROM THE HILLS TO THE COAST THEY TOOK BACK OUR LAND
FOR LIBERTY'S SAKE THEY TOOK A BOLD STAND
OUR NATION WAS BORN BY THE TEAM AND THE SCHEME
OF MARION SUMTER PICKENS AND GREENE

TO THANK THESE GREAT LEADERS AND HONOR GREENE'S SKILL
OUR TOWN AND OUR COUNTY WERE CHRISTENED GREENEVILLE!

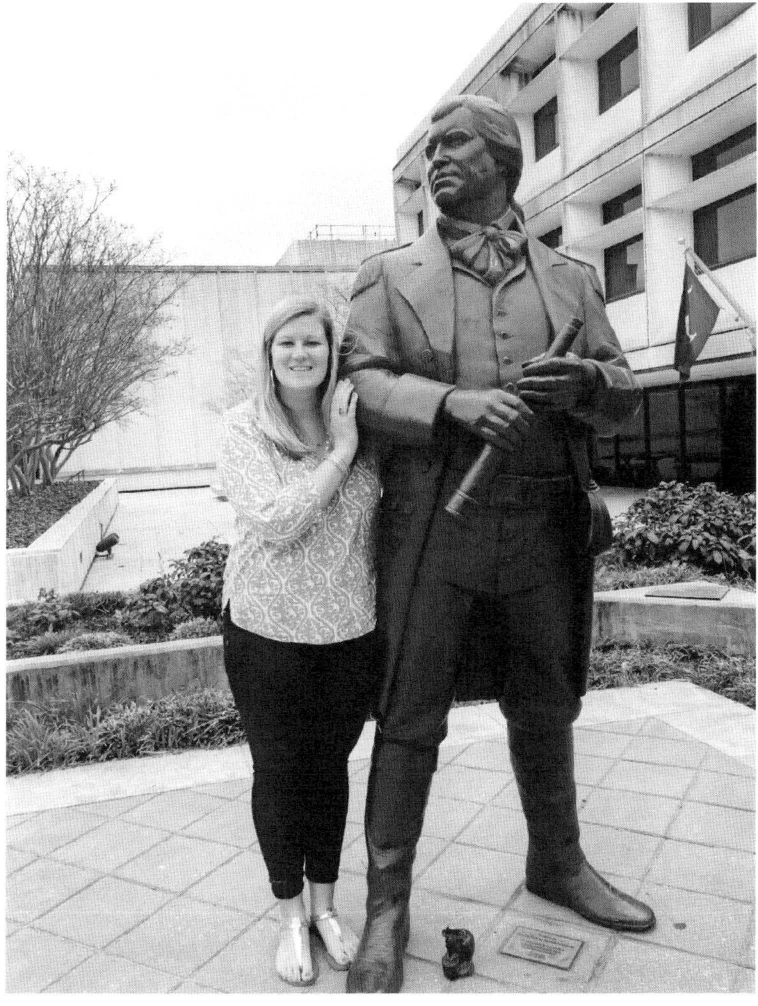

Author posing with statue of General Nathanael Greene in downtown Greenville, South Carolina. *Photo by Manning Mullikin.*

least been honored with several towns and landmarks named after him, such as many Greene Counties in different states and the towns of Greene, Greenville and Greensboro also in several states.

Greene was meticulous and wary as a general; he never launched into any risky attacks and always kept a level head, as he had a clear goal in mind. His attitude as a military commander was similar to that of his participation in public policy debates, as he confidently fought the British with politics as well as artillery as he successfully pushed them down into Charleston and eventually out altogether. Greene knew everything there was to know about the military and was meticulous in all of his endeavors, which is why he was ultimately successful despite never actually winning a battle in the tactical sense. He was well liked, and his fellow officers respected him as a careful and studied leader. He managed to keep his demoralized and poorly equipped army together to fend off the British, Loyalists and armed slaves. In his final months as commander, Greene was constantly moving, engaging with the enemy, solving supply and personal deficits, taking political action and keeping his military focused on its task. Greene's forgotten and overlooked 1782 campaign finally earned him the strategic triumph over the British, as well as his place as one of the great general officers of the Revolution, that he richly deserved.

NOTES

Introduction

1. Conrad, *July–December 1781*, vol. 9, *Papers of General Nathanael Greene* (hereafter *PNG*).
2. Greene to Caty Greene, September 4, 1781, *PNG* 9:336.
3. Carbone, *Nathanael Greene*, 203.
4. Williams to Greene, September 9, 1781, *PNG* 9:334.
5. Greene to Washington, September 11, 1781, *PNG* 9:329.
6. Rankin and Scheer, *Rebels and Redcoats*, 464.
7. Greene to Rutledge, September 9, 1781, *PNG* 9:308.
8. Carbone, *Nathanael Greene*, 206.
9. Ibid.

Chapter 1

10. See Stegeman and Stegeman, *Caty*.
11. Golway, *Washington's General*, 2.
12. Ibid.
13. Ibid., 4.
14. Washington to Greene, October 5, 1780, quoted in Conrad, "Nathanael Greene and the Southern Campaigns," 1.
15. Anderson, *Forgotten Patriot*, 1.
16. Borick, *Gallant Defense*, 6.
17. Ibid., 10.
18. Conrad, "Nathanael Greene and the Southern Campaigns," 5.

19. Ibid., 2.
20. Benjamin Lincoln to George Washington, December 19, 1778, quoted in Shipton, "Benjamin Lincoln," 198.
21. Conrad, "Nathanael Greene and the Southern Campaigns," 4.
22. Frey, *Water from the Rock*, 117.
23. Piecuch, *Three Peoples, One King*, 290.
24. Haw, "Every Thing Here Depends Upon Opinion," 31.

Chapter 2

25. Conrad, "Nathanael Greene and the Southern Campaigns," iii.
26. Ibid., iv.
27. Ibid., v.
28. Ibid., 1.
29. Jasanoff, *Liberty's Exiles*, 53.
30. Conrad, "Nathanael Greene and the Southern Campaigns," 50.
31. Greene to Jefferson, December 6, 1780, quoted in Conrad, "Nathanael Greene and the Southern Campaigns," 101.
32. Greene to Joseph Reed, January 9, 1781, quoted in Conrad, "Nathanael Greene and the Southern Campaigns," 102.
33. Conrad, "Nathanael Greene and the Southern Campaigns," 55.
34. Ibid., 33.
35. Ibid., 72.
36. Greene to Washington, December 28, 1780, quoted in Conrad, "Nathanael Greene and the Southern Campaigns," 73.
37. Conrad, "Nathanael Greene and the Southern Campaigns," 102.
38. Tarleton to Cornwallis, January 4, 1781, in Tarleton, *History of the Campaign*, 246.
39. Tarleton, *History of the Campaign*, 248–49.
40. Ibid., 221.
41. Ibid., 218.
42. Conrad, "Nathanael Greene and the Southern Campaigns," 107.
43. Greene to Marion, January 25, 1781, quoted in Conrad, "Nathanael Greene and the Southern Campaigns," 161.
44. Greene to John Matthews, January, 23, 1781, quoted in Conrad, "Nathanael Greene and the Southern Campaigns," 164.

Chapter 3

45. Conrad, "Nathanael Greene and the Southern Campaigns," 142.
46. Ibid., 144.

47. Lee, *Memoirs of the War*, 263.
48. Conrad, "Nathanael Greene and the Southern Campaigns," 153.
49. Greene to Morgan, March 20, 1781, quoted in Conrad, "Nathanael Greene and the Southern Campaigns," 154.
50. Conrad, "Nathanael Greene and the Southern Campaigns," 164.
51. Greene to Steuben, April 3, 1781, quoted in Conrad, "Nathanael Greene and the Southern Campaigns," 243.
52. Conrad, "Nathanael Greene and the Southern Campaigns," 177.
53. Ibid., 185.
54. Greene to Huntington, May 5, 1781, quoted in Conrad, "Nathanael Greene and the Southern Campaigns," 205.
55. Conrad, "Nathanael Greene and the Southern Campaigns," 221.
56. Greene to the president of Congress, June 9, 1781, quoted in Conrad, "Nathanael Greene and the Southern Campaigns," 228.
57. Greene to Sumter, June 10, 1781, quoted in Conrad, "Nathanael Greene and the Southern Campaigns," 244.
58. Greene to Arthur St. Clair, June 22, 1781; Greene to Francis Locke, June 21, 1781, quoted in Conrad, "Nathanael Greene and the Southern Campaigns," 245.
59. Conrad, "Nathanael Greene and the Southern Campaigns," 236.
60. Ibid., 241.
61. Greene to Catharine Greene, July 18, 1781, *PNG* 9:35.
62. Greene to Thomas McKean, July 17, 1781, *PNG* 9:27–30.

Chapter 4

63. Conrad, "Nathanael Greene and the Southern Campaigns," 245.
64. Tarleton, *History of the Campaign*, 524.
65. Greene to Marion, September 5, 1781, *PNG* 9:298.
66. Tarleton, *History of the Campaign*, 524.
67. Conrad, "Nathanael Greene and the Southern Campaigns," 248.
68. Ibid., 250.
69. Greene to Washington, September 11, 1781, *PNG* 9:329.
70. Lee, *Memoirs of the War*, 469.
71. Conrad, "Nathanael Greene and the Southern Campaigns," 252.
72. Greene to Washington, September 11, 1781, *PNG* 9:328.
73. Conrad, "Nathanael Greene and the Southern Campaigns," 254.
74. Greene to the president of Congress, September 11, 1781, *PNG* 9:322.
75. Greene to George Washington, September 17, 1781, *PNG* 9:351.
76. Conrad, "Nathanael Greene and the Southern Campaigns," 257.
77. Greene to Harry Lee, October 1, 1781, *PNG* 9:409.

78. Greene to Lafayette, September 17, 1781, *PNG* 9:356.
79. Ramsay, *History of the American Revolution*, 2:255.
80. Greene to the president of Congress, October 25, 1781, *PNG* 9:483.
81. Robert Morris to Greene, September 10, 1781, *PNG* 9:310.

Chapter 5

82. Greene to Burke, August 12, 1781, *PNG* 9:166.
83. Greene to Rutherford, October 20, 1781, *PNG* 9:465.
84. Rutherford to Greene, December 10, 1781, *PNG* 10:32.
85. Jasanoff, *Liberty's Exiles*, 56.
86. Greene to Arthur St. Clair, November 24, 1781, *PNG* 9:611.
87. Jasanoff, *Liberty's Exiles*, 55.
88. Greene to Washington, September 9, 1781, *PNG* 9:312.
89. Greene to Lafayette, October 8, 1781, *PNG* 9:436.
90. Conrad, "Nathanael Greene and the Southern Campaigns," 1979.
91. Williams to Greene, October 10, 1781, *PNG* 9:449.
92. Greene to Marion, November 2, 1781, *PNG* 9:521.
93. Greene to Washington, November 21, 1781, *PNG* 9:604.
94. Marion to Greene, November 14, 1781, *PNG* 9:573. Marion guessed that the British would go down to Georgia and evacuate South Carolina because they could not possibly need that many slaves in Charleston. Marion was incorrect about the British evacuating South Carolina, as they stayed for another year.
95. Frey, *Water from the Rock*, 122.
96. Marion to Greene, November 25, 1781, *PNG* 9:628.
97. Marion to Greene, November 30, 1781, *PNG* 9:621.
98. Greene to Thomas Sumter, December 2, 1781, *PNG* 9:630. Greene thought that the British had acted respectfully because they left their posts at Dorchester and Goose Creek without putting up a fight.
99. Greene to Williams, December 2, 1781, *PNG* 9:631.
100. Conrad, "Nathanael Greene and the Southern Campaigns," 273.
101. Johnson, *Sketches of the Life*, 2:266.
102. Piecuch, *Three Peoples, One King*, 310.
103. Ibid., 309.
104. Massey, *John Laurens and the American Revolution*, 206.
105. Haw, "Every Thing Here Depends Upon Opinion," 231.
106. Greene to Reed, July 18, 1782, *PNG* 11:449.
107. Greene to Gist, August 15, 1782, *PNG* 11:547; Marion to Greene, August 23, 1782, *PNG* 11:571; Marion to Greene, August 27, 1782, *PNG* 11:583. Commands of Greene to Marion and Gist show constant motion but few casualties.

108. Marion to Greene, January 1, 1782, *PNG* 10:147.
109. Greene to Lee, December 27, 1781, *PNG* 10:111.
110. Washington to Greene, February 1, 1782, *PNG* 10:290.
111. Conrad, "Nathanael Greene and the Southern Campaigns," 301.
112. Greene to Rutledge, May 14, 1781, quoted in Conrad, "Nathanael Greene and the Southern Campaigns," 301. When Rutledge left for Philadelphia, he put Greene in charge. As military leader, he made many executive decisions.
113. Henrietta Wragg to Greene, January 7, 1782, *PNG* 10:167. Greene's reply has not been found.
114. Greene to Marion, January 16, 1782, *PNG* 10:202.
115. Greene to Sumter, January 8, 1782, *PNG* 10:168.

Chapter 6

116. Greene to Rutledge, January 16, 1782, *PNG* 10:206. The British commander reported that they left on their own accord and doubted that the Patriot expedition would have forced them to leave Johns Island.
117. Greene to Washington, January 24, 1782, *PNG* 10:257.
118. Piecuch, *Three Peoples, One King*, 290.
119. Ibid., 318.
120. Conrad, "Nathanael Greene and the Southern Campaigns," 307.
121. Frey, *Water from the Rock*, 117.
122. Massey, *John Laurens and the American Revolution*, 207.
123. Greene to Rutledge, December 9, 1781, *PNG* 10:21.
124. Piecuch, *Three Peoples, One King*, 333.
125. Greene to Washington, March 9, 1782, *PNG* 10:472.
126. Maham to Greene, November 27, 1781, *PNG* 9:620.
127. Ramsay, *History of the Revolution in South-Carolina*, 277.
128. Greene to Balfour, August 26, 1781, *PNG* 9:249.
129. Horry to Greene, February 28, 1782, *PNG* 10:419. Horry was actually not present at this skirmish, as he was sick. He left Major Benison in charge, and Benison was killed during the conflict.
130. Rutledge to Marion, September 16, 1781, *PNG* 9:336.
131. Greene to Marion, December 12, 1781, *PNG* 10:38.
132. Greene to John Martin, January 9, 1782, *PNG* 10:173.
133. Conrad, "Nathanael Greene and the Southern Campaigns," 317.
134. Jasanoff, *Liberty's Exiles*, 68.
135. Greene to Reed, February 27, 1782, *PNG* 10:414.
136. Leslie to Greene, April 4, 1782, *PNG* 10:583.
137. Jasanoff, *Liberty's Exiles*, 69.

138. Ibid.
139. Greene to the president of Congress, August 29, 1782, *PNG* 11:591.
140. Greene, General Orders, August 30, 1782, *PNG* 11:602.
141. Massey, *John Laurens and the American Revolution*, 228.
142. Greene to the president of Congress, May 18, 1782, *PNG* 11:200; Greene to the president of Congress, July 10, 1782, *PNG* 11:433.
143. Greene to Lee, October 7, 1862, *PNG* 12:41.
144. Richard Henry Lee to Greene, October 5, 1862, *PNG* 12:30.
145. Greene to John Mathews, November 18, 1782, *PNG* 12:205.
146. Greene to Major Alexander Roxburgh, November 21, 1782, *PNG* 12:209.
147. Greene to Marion, November 22, 1782, *PNG* 12:211.
148. Greene to the president of Congress, December 19, 1782, *PNG* 12:301.
149. Barnwell, "Evacuation of Charleston by the British in 1782," 19–21.

Epilogue

150. Conrad, "Nathanael Greene and the Southern Campaigns," 323–24.
151. Guerard to Greene, March 7, 1783, *PNG* 12:494; Greene to Guerard, March 9, 1783, *PNG* 12:498.
152. Conrad, "Nathanael Greene and the Southern Campaigns," 327.
153. Greene to Guerard, March 8, 1783, *PNG* 12:498.
154. Greene to Otho Williams, April 11, 1783, *PNG* 12:598.
155. Greene to Robert Morris, April 20, 1783, *PNG* 12:623.

BIBLIOGRAPHY

Primary Sources

Caldwell, Charles. *Memoirs of the Life and Campaigns of the Hon. Nathanael Greene.* Philadelphia: Robert DeSilver and Thomas DeSilver, 1819.

Clinton, Sir Henry. *The American Rebellion: Sir Henry Clinton's Narrative of His Campaigns, 1775–1782.* Edited by William B. Wilcox. New Haven, CT: Yale University Press, 1954.

Conrad, Dennis M., ed. *April–September 1782*. Vol. 11 of *The Papers of General Nathanael Greene*. Chapel Hill: University of North Carolina Press, 1997.

———. *December 1781–April 1782*. Vol. 10 of *The Papers of General Nathanael Greene*. Chapel Hill: University of North Carolina Press, 1997.

———. *July–December 1781*. Vol. 9 of *The Papers of General Nathanael Greene.* Chapel Hill: University of North Carolina Press, 1997.

———. *October 1782–May 1783*. Vol. 12 of *The Papers of General Nathanael Greene*. Chapel Hill: University of North Carolina Press, 1997.

Lee, Henry. *Memoirs of the War in the Southern Department of the United States.* Philadelphia: Bradford and Irskeep, 1812.

Martin, Joseph Plumb. *A Narrative of a Revolutionary Soldier: Some of the Adventures, Misgivings, and Sufferings of Joseph Plumb Martin.* Reprint, New York: Signet Classic, 2001. Originally published in 1830.

Tarleton, Banastre. *History of the Campaign of 1780 and 1781 in the Southern Provinces of North America*. Dublin: printed for Colles, 1787.

Secondary Literature

Anderson, Lee. *Forgotten Patriot: The Life and Times of Major-General Nathanael Greene*. New York: Universal Publishers, 2002.

Barnwell, Joseph W. "The Evacuation of Charleston by the British in 1782." *South Carolina Historical and Genealogical Magazine* 11, no. 1 (January 1910): 1–26.

Borick, Carl. *A Gallant Defense: The Siege of Charleston, 1780*. Columbia: University of South Carolina Press, 2003.

Buchanan, John. *The Road to Guilford Courthouse: The American Revolution in the Carolinas*. New York: John Wiley & Sons, 1997.

Carbone, Gerald M. *Nathanael Greene: A Biography of the American Revolution*. New York: Palgrave Macmillan, 2008.

Conrad, Dennis M. "Nathanael Greene and the Southern Campaigns, 1780–1783." PhD diss., Duke University, 1979.

Dederer, John Morgan. *Making Bricks Without Straw: Nathanael Greene's Southern Campaign and Mao Tse-tung's Mobile War*. Manhattan, KS: Sunflower University Press, 1983.

Edgar, Walter. *Partisans and Redcoats: The Southern Conflict that Turned the Tide of the American Revolution*. New York: HarperCollins Publishers, 2001.

Frey, Silvia. *Water from the Rock: Black Resistance in a Revolutionary Age*. Princeton, NJ: Princeton University Press, 1992.

Golway, Terry. *Washington's General: Nathanael Greene and the Triumph of the American Revolution*. New York: Owl Books, 2006.

Gordon, John. *South Carolina and the American Revolution: A Battlefield History*. Columbia: University of South Carolina Press, 2003.

Haw, James. "'Every Thing Here Depends Upon Opinion': Nathanael Greene and Public Support in the Southern Campaigns of the American Revolution." *South Carolina Historical Magazine* 109 (July 2008): 212–31.

Jasanoff, Maya. *Liberty's Exiles: American Loyalists in the Revolutionary*. New York: Random House Inc., 2011.

Johnson, William. *Sketches of the Life and Correspondence of Nathanael Greene*. 2 vols. Charleston, SC: A.E. Miller, 1822.

Lumpkin, Henry. *From Savannah to Yorktown: The American Revolution in the South*. Columbia: University of South Carolina Press, 1981.

Massey, Gregory D. *John Laurens and the American Revolution*. Columbia: University of South Carolina Press, 2000.

Massey, Gregory D., and Jim Piecuch, eds. *General Nathanael Greene and the American Revolution in the South*. Columbia: University of South Carolina Press, 2012.

McCrady, Edward. *The History of South Carolina, 1775–1780*. New York: Macmillan Company, 1901.

Pancake, John. *This Destructive War: The British Campaign in the Carolinas, 1780–1782*. Tuscaloosa: University of Alabama Press, 1985.

Piecuch, Jim. *Three Peoples, One King: Loyalists, Indians, and Slaves in the Revolutionary South*. Columbia: University of South Carolina Press, 2008.

Ramsay, David. *History of the American Revolution*. Philadelphia: R. Aitken and Son, 1789.

———. *The History of the Revolution of South-Carolina, from a British Province to an Independent State*. N.p.: Trenton, 1785.

Rankin, Hugh, and George Scheer. *Rebels and Redcoats: The American Revolution Through the Eyes of Those Who Fought and Lived It*. New York: Da Capo Press, 1957.

Shipton, Clifford K. "Benjamin Lincoln: Old Reliable." In *George Washington's Generals*. Edited by George Alton Billias. New York, 1964.

Stegeman, John F., and Janet A. Stegeman. *Caty: A Biography of Catharine Littlefield Greene*. Athens, GA: Brown Thrasher Books, 1985.

Ulhar, Janet. *Freedom's Cost: The Story of General Nathanael Greene*. Indianapolis, IN: Dog Ear Publishing, 2011.

INDEX

ABOUT THE AUTHOR

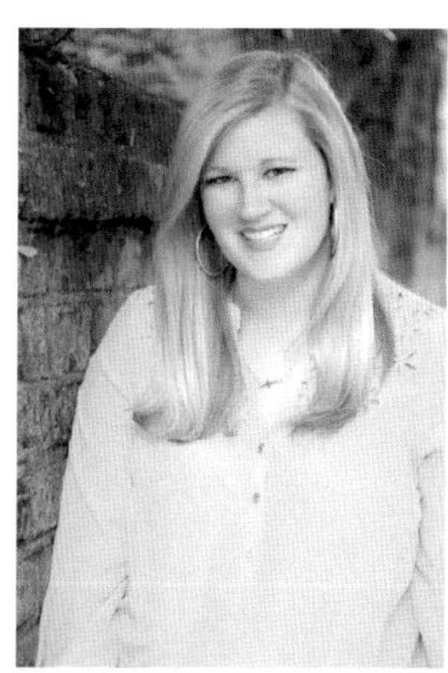

Leigh Moring is the Education Coordinator for Historic Charleston Foundation, where she manages K-12 educational programming in historic house museums. She attended Clemson University and received her Bachelor of Arts in history with a concentration in public history. Moring went on to pursue her Master of Arts degree in history from the College of Charleston and The Citadel and graduated in May 2015. She has worked in several museums and historic sites in South Carolina and is enjoying living in and exploring Charleston with her friends.

Visit us at
www.historypress.net

This title is also available as an e-book